ON THE EDGE
OF FLIGHT

The time will come when thou shalt lift thine eyes,
To watch a long drawn battle in the skies,
While aged peasants too amazed for words,
Stare at the flying fleets of wondrous birds.
England, so long the mistress of the sea,
Where wind and waves confess her sovereignty,
Her ancient triumphs yet on high shall bear,
And reign, the sovereign of the conquered air.

(Translated from Grays 'Lunar Habitalis', Cambridge 1737)

ON THE EDGE OF FLIGHT

A Lifetime in the Development and Engineering of Aircraft

Eric Absolon

C.Eng. FRAeS. F.Eng.Inst.

Pen & Sword
AVIATION

First published in Great Britain by
PEN AND SWORD AVIATION
an imprint of
Pen and Sword Books Ltd
47 Church Street
Barnsley
South Yorkshire S70 2AS

ISBN 978 1 78159 077 5

A CIP record for this book is available from the British Library.

Printed and bound in England by
CPI Group (UK) Ltd, Croydon, CR0 4YY

Typeset in Times by CHIC GRAPHICS

Pen & Sword Books Ltd incorporates the imprints of
Pen & Sword Aviation, Pen & Sword Family History, Pen & Sword Maritime,
Pen & Sword Military, Pen & Sword Discovery, Wharncliffe Local History,
Wharncliffe True Crime, Wharncliffe Transport, Pen & Sword Select,
Pen & Sword Military Classics, Leo Cooper, Remember When,
The Praetorian Press, Seaforth Publishing and Frontline Publishing

For a complete list of Pen and Sword titles please contact
Pen and Sword Books Limited
47 Church Street, Barnsley, South Yorkshire, S70 2AS, England
E-mail: enquiries@pen-and-sword.co.uk
Website: www.pen-and-sword.co.uk

Contents

Dedication

T est flying tends to be looked upon as a glamorous occupation. Dashing young men carrying out dare-devil acts in the sky to check out new aeroplanes.

The reality is quite different. By and large, these are dedicated, qualified, people carrying out a meticulous and detailed job to a flight schedule carefully planned and executed. A schedule designed, over a number of organised missions, to explore the aircraft characteristics over the designed flight envelope.

But sometimes things go wrong. Much of this book is about the fourteen years that I spent in engineering research at Gloster Aircraft Co. Probably the most demanding, exciting and formative years of my life. During that time, very sadly, five test pilots lost their lives.

This book is dedicated to their memories –

Gloster Test Pilot, Lieutenant. J. Bridge. Meteor stalled on final approach.
Gloster Test Pilot, Rodney Dryland. Meteor disintegrated during high speed run over airfield.
Gloster Test Pilot, Peter Lawrence. Javelin, failed to recover from stall (see Chapter 1)
RAE Pilot, attached to Glosters. Flight. Lieutenant Ross. Javelin. Failed to recover from spin.
Gloster Test Pilot Brian Smith. Javelin, mid-air collision with Hunter.

Author's note.

This book has been written to appeal (hopefully) to those not necessarily familiar with aviation theory and terminology, not the least of which are the author's children and grandchildren.

Therefore, it is hoped that those that are familiar and, indeed, expert in such matters will forgive the simplified expressions, diagrams and explanations. Also, please remember that the events described took place over fifty years ago and aeronautical science has moved on. New theories, new ideas, new technology, new ways of expressing experienced phenomena. But history is important and the author believes it important to record the earlier struggles.

Introduction

S ince man first staggered into the air in early flying machines, incredibly fragile and, by today's standards, grossly under-powered with unreliable engines, he has relentlessly pursued the quest for higher speeds and greater carrying capacity. Urged on by marginal improvements by competition and, with the dawning of the commercial travel age, the race to meet the increasing demands of emerging airlines, a great industry struggled through labour and into birth.

Sadly, some of the most rapid advances were made during two world wars to meet the needs of defence and offence operational requirements. This continued to be true during the period of the Cold War, with vastly increased technology emerging and the advent of sophisticated early warning systems and guided weapons.

More speed, more load, more range, more altitude, more manoeuverability, was the continual demand from the armed services, passed on by the Ministry of Defence, with specifications issued in the form of an O.R. – an Operational Requirement.

Their needs were met, with varying degrees of success, by teams of designers, engineers, pilots, administrators, continually striving to improve their product and at the same time to create a successful business. The aircraft industry in Britain had been wholly one of private venture, founded on the dreams of individual men and the commercial viability of their enterprises, backed by government research establishments such as the Royal Aircraft Establishment at Farnborough.

The quest for speed took a sharp up-turn during the Second World War and aircraft evolved from the early Schneider Trophy machines, tailored to specific military needs. The Spitfire and Hurricane of course being perhaps the best known, but followed by many others in rapid succession.

Soon, the aerodynamicists began to think seriously about the magic speed of sound – about 760mph at sea level. It was known that many of the classic aerodynamic laws by which aircraft were designed would have to be modified in this speed range, where suddenly air was no longer a predictable incompressible medium. At the speed of sound, disturbances in the air would

INTRODUCTION

no longer travel ahead of the aircraft. They would stay with it, creating shock waves and changes in pressure distribution and airflow that were largely unknown and unpredictable.

Later versions of piston engines aircraft had reached speeds of 500-600mph in dives and already pilots had experienced dramatic effects of trim change, buffeting, stick shake and some degree of control reversal. With the advent of the jet engine and previously undreamed of power available the popularly christened "sound barrier" became a reality. We began to talk in terms of Mach No - the ratio of the speed of flight to the speed of sound through the air at the particular altitude and temperature condition being encountered. The magic number was one - Mach 1 and beyond. If a further step forward in speed was to be obtained, this target had to be reached and the unknown become the known and the familiar.

So, the quest was on. It sounds over dramatic to say it was probing the unknown, but this is what it was. It occupied the period roughly from 1946 to 1960 and absorbed the energies and talents of many distinguished designers and aerodynamicists and the lives of a number of brave men, the test pilots and observers without whose skills and bravery nothing would be accomplished. The post war peace was uneasy during this time, resting precariously on a balance of power. Defence needs acted as the spur, which created an aircraft industry in Britain at its peak and probably, at that time, the best in the world. Sadly, it has now changed irrevocably and can never be the same again. One time airfields fallen in to disuse, concrete covered in grass and weeds, great factories turned into trading estates. Individual enterprises now swallowed up into large conglomerates manufacturing only parts of aircraft now so large and complex that no one individual team can conceive and manage the project.

Such is the passage of history, "The moving finger, having writ, moves on." But it was an immense and exciting period that will be remembered by many with affectionate nostalgia. These pages record some of those times, based on the author's own involvement during this period, multiplied many times by the efforts of others. Some recorded for ever in history, some forgotten in the mists of time, but all forming an endeavour unique in history and not likely to be seen again.

These tales are the memories of one man exposed to the thrill of aviation and everything to do with aircraft, models or real, from a very early age and throughout a busy, dedicated and interesting – nay – intensely exciting life.

Chapter 1

The Loss of
Peter Lawrence

The small knot of people gathered by the hangar door, fitters, some office staff, a couple of visitors, all wondering. Where was Peter Lawrence? What had happened? It was a routine test flight on the second Javelin prototype WD808 wasn't it? Or was it?

The only message had been 'I'm in trouble'. Nothing else. Wasn't even known exactly where he was. Test flights were normally conducted over the Bristol Channel, away from land and housing, just in case. Bill Waterton, Chief Test Pilot, took off in a Meteor that was flight ready, to go and have a look round – Peter was now well overdue. The little group waited in silence. Peter Lawrence was popular, treated everyone with courtesy – fitters, staff, executives, all the same. Very professional in his work and dedicated to the testing and improvement of our aeroplane, the Javelin.

The Meteor came into view, circled and landed. Bill Waterton taxied right up to where the group waited, shut down engines, climbed down and walked across. 'He's down, just by Flax Bourton, there's been a fire – just wreckage left.'

There was silence. Little wisps of wind on a calm day blew a few leaves, a scrap of paper rustled, otherwise silence. Nobody moved. 'Oh! F... that,' from Nobby Clark, one of the team that prepared aircraft for flight, his mind wondering already – why? What happened?

Most test flying is routine, performing manoeuvres, exploring flight envelopes to programmes set out by the aerodynamicists and engineers, each flight carefully planned and executed to prove a design parameter, with recordings made of everything relevant during the flight.

But, in this case, not quite so routine. There were some problems with the aircraft to be resolved, as with most early prototypes of a new design.

Bill Waterton, it seemed, was being very cautious about moving ahead too quickly into the full flight envelope.

The Javelin was an early example of what is known as Delta wing configuration with an 'all moving tailplane'. That is to say, the wing form is like a triangle, which gives it a large area with a swept back leading edge. This is for two reasons. The Javelin was an all weather interceptor aircraft, designed to meet Air Ministry specification F4/48. The specification called for operation at high altitude, where the air density is very low. (At 55,000ft air density is only about one eighth of ground level density.) An aircraft relies on air acting on its wing surface to hold it up. In general terms, the lift force to maintain flight is a function of the forward speed, the air density, the wing area and a lift coefficient. Again, in very general terms, the lift coefficient is a function of the 'angle of attack' of the wing to the air stream. The shape of the wing section, combined with the angle of attack to the air stream, causes the air flow to accelerate over the top of the wing and slow down underneath. This is demonstrated by the diagrammatic streamlines shown in the diagram.

By a fundamental law of aerodynamics, when airflow is increased in this manner, the pressure drops and, conversely when airflow is reduced, pressure increases. This is shown by the change in spacing of the streamlines

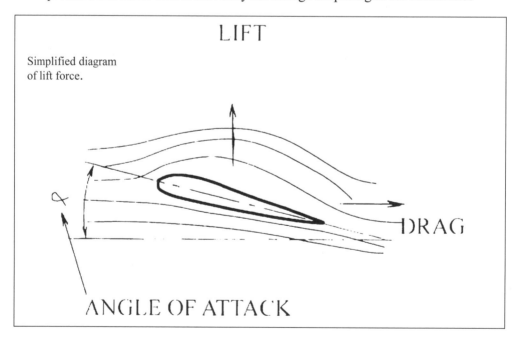

LIFT

Simplified diagram
of lift force.

DRAG

ANGLE OF ATTACK

in the diagram. Therefore, it can be seen, there will be a pressure difference between the lower and upper surfaces of the wing. The pressure under the wing is higher than the pressure on the upper side and, therefore, there is a resultant lift force on the wing.

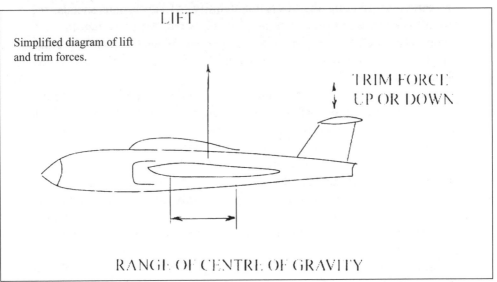

LIFT

Simplified diagram of lift and trim forces.

TRIM FORCE
UP OR DOWN

RANGE OF CENTRE OF GRAVITY

As we have seen above, at altitude the air density dramatically reduces. But, of course, the weight of the aircraft stays the same, whatever the altitude. Therefore, to stay in the air, the angle of attack has to *progressively increase* until the aircraft is at the stall. The combination of these factors determines the maximum height, or ceiling, that the aircraft can attain. Further, to maintain manoeuvrability at high altitude and to be an effective fighting machine capable of intercepting and destroying enemy aircraft, low wing loading is desirable. Therefore, for all these reasons, a large wing area resulted. The swept back leading edge of the wing came about because this was the time of exploring supersonic flight and there was much talk of the so called 'sound barrier'. Not actually a barrier at all, but a rapid build-up of aerodynamic drag as the aircraft approaches the speed of sound in the air conditions it is experiencing at the time. Nothing to do with sound as such, simply the speed at which pressure waves are transmitted through the air medium. This is, of course, the same speed at which sound is transmitted, being no more than pressure waves.

At subsonic speeds, the pressure disturbances caused by the aircraft's movement through the air, travel away from the front of the aircraft, because they are moving at a greater speed than the aircraft. As the aircraft approaches the speed of sound however, this can no longer happen and a pressure wave builds up in front of the wing causing very high drag forces accompanied by rapid changes in the centre of pressure on the wing, thus dramatically affecting the aircraft's stability. At supersonic speeds, the aircraft is travelling faster than the pressure wave, which is therefore left behind as a shock wave radiating in all directions. When this hits the ground, effectively as a sound wave, it creates the 'super-sonic bang' heard by any observer in its path.

The transition from subsonic to supersonic flight is therefore accompanied by a large increase in the power required, due to the very high drag forces. But also, accompanied by rapid changes in the way in which the aerodynamic forces act on the aircraft wing. For example, as already mentioned, the centre of pressure will rapidly change, causing changes in aircraft trim. Sweeping back the leading edge of the wing delays the onset of the build-up of drag and the trim and stability changes that take place. Hence the triangular, or Delta wing form, was born as a means of operating at the highest possible subsonic speed at high altitude with maximum manoeuvrability.

Supersonic flight is now routine, with high powered engines capable of overcoming the drag forces, coupled with advanced aerodynamics applied to the aircraft design. But that was not so at the time of the Javelin. Much was unknown. To this day, supersonic flight is only achievable at the expense of disproportionate power and fuel consumption. This is why all civilian aircraft operate in the high subsonic speed range. Concorde was a very special case, with operating costs that meant it only ever attracted those prepared to pay a high price to travel. Also, of course, very limited on routes because of the environmental impact of the sonic bang over land. Anyone who heard Concorde passing over when going down the channel would understand that!

So, the Javelin was evolved with a large Delta wing plan form. But what about the tail plane and elevators? These provide pitch control and obviously need to be as far back as possible to give best control and clear of aerodynamic disturbances from the wing. The answer on the Javelin was to place it high up above the rudder and fin, where it would meet clear air and give optimum control.

Unfortunately, this was to create a problem completely unforeseen and partially resulting in the tragedy of Peter Lawrence.

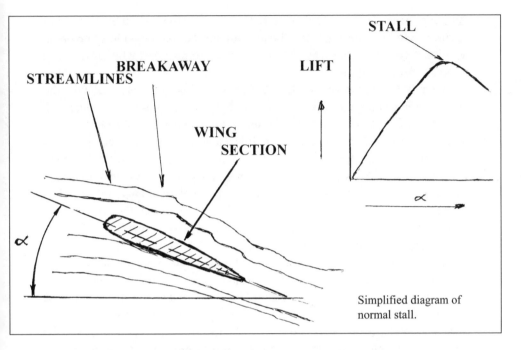

STALL

BREAKAWAY
STREAMLINES

LIFT

WING
SECTION

Simplified diagram of
normal stall.

Exploring high speed flight is one thing, but any aircraft also has to perform safely at low speeds and there is a point at which the forward speed will no longer produce the lift to keep the aircraft in the air – the stall.

The photograph is interesting in this respect. It shows a Gladiator, Meteor and Javelin, in formation, at the same speed. The Gladiator is probably close to its design maximum speed and therefore at a very small angle of attack. The Meteor has a moderate angle. But the Javelin is probably close to the stall, with a high angle of attack needed to generate the lift required to stay in the air.

Because of the reduction in air density, the greater the altitude, the closer the stall speed becomes to the maximum speed the aircraft can achieve at that altitude. This is because, although the drag is reduced due to the lower air density, so also is the thrust from the engine and, eventually, the maximum forward speed equals the stall speed and the aircraft has reached its limit. Clearly, therefore, for a high altitude interceptor fighter, this is a most important area to be explored in flight testing. But the characteristics of the stall are important at any altitude. In particular, the ability to recover from an unintentional stall.

When the message came, 'I'm in trouble', Peter Lawrence was doing just that, exploring the aircraft characteristics close to the stall at an altitude of 12,500ft. He lowered flaps and the aircraft stalled, but apparently he could not effect recovery – but why? More than that, much more, why did he leave it too late to eject safely?

After the initial shock of Bill Waterton's message, 'He's down', the organisation swung into action. There would be full enquiries, investigations, collection of evidence, meetings, conferences and an eventual determination of what happened. Except that, in this case, there was never any real satisfactory explanation as to why Peter Lawrence left it too late to eject. Until very recently, when the author came across some evidence that may well offer a solution to the mystery, as will be explained later.

At that time, however, for those immediately involved, they must know now. Is there anything, anything at all, we might see – something to do with the special apparatus fitted to the aircraft for flight testing perhaps? Something to do with the controls and the tests and modifications carried out? For those of us directly involved, these were pressing matters. We had to know, to see with our own eyes before the wreckage is disturbed. And then there are the records. All flight testing is monitored by automatic observers, recording every aspect of the aircraft's movement, controls, throttle setting etc. Nowadays we have highly sophisticated observers with telemetry and so on. In those days we had mostly camera recordings of instruments and chart recorders, all of which had to be recovered from the aircraft.

A small group of the most vitally interested people, including the author, travelled by car to the scene of the accident, where the Javelin came down. A sight never to be forgotten.

There was our aircraft, in a corner of a field, lying flat on the ground. I say 'our aircraft' because that is the way in which we thought of the prototypes. Working with them, living with them, becoming attached as a living, dynamic mechanism, but at the same time a beautiful flying machine. And there it was now, a dead piece of wreckage. There had been a fire in the centre section which was burnt out. It looked as though the automatic fire extinguishers had dealt with that and stopped it spreading, but the cockpit area was completely destroyed.

The whole aircraft had collapsed and folded itself to the ground as though a large invisible force had pushed downwards over the whole 'plane and tried to force it into the earth. The fuselage and wing structure were in contact over their whole area. The field was grass and blades of grass were still vertical within an inch of the trailing edge of the wing – not bent or bruised, just growing straight upwards. It was obvious that whatever else had happened, the aircraft had hit the ground with no forward speed whatsoever.

It is hard to convey the sense of loss and desolation in seeing this wonderful flying machine, potentially capable of so many things; low speed, high speed, aerobatics, low level passes, rapid climbs to unheard of altitudes; and now, just lying there, a dead piece of wreckage.

But, much more important, what of Peter Lawrence? The police were already on the scene of course. The ambulance had come and gone, their job done. But not quite. It appeared that Peter Lawrence had ejected too late. He was found still in the seat, not far from the aircraft. I was walking around the scene, trying to think what might have happened, wondering about the controls, wondering why did it come straight down, no forward speed. Why couldn't it be controlled?

There, not far from the aircraft, were some small pieces the ambulance crew had not cleaned up.

Try to come to terms with this. This was a man who struggled with this Javelin, who stayed with it and ejected too late. This was a vital, living being, a team with his aeroplane; and this is what's left? A small piece of human remains, strangely fresh and in some odd way, living but yet dead.

Ambulance crews and police at accident scenes must be familiar with such sights. But for me, essentially at the scene for technical reasons, this was something to be faced. A machine crashed. We have to know why, what happened, a thousand questions, mind racing; the controls? hydraulics? And others there will be thinking of other possibilities. The engineers and technicians will immediately focus on systems – mechanical, hydraulic, electrical. But the aerodynamicists will be thinking of aerodynamics, the structural engineers, of structures. Did something break? Was something not strong enough for the manoeuvres being performed?

But above all this, regardless of what may or may not have happened, a man lay dead. This is what is left. It seemed an eternity contemplating this small piece of what was humanity. In reality probably only minutes. Getting it into perspective. Thoughts of life and death. Only a few hours ago I saw this dynamic, vibrant man climb into his aircraft. And now this.

Never mind about anything else. This man died and he shouldn't have done. Why?

Records later removed from the wreckage showed all too clearly something of what must have happened. At that time various forms of automatic observer were used to record everything taking place on the

WD808 flight records.

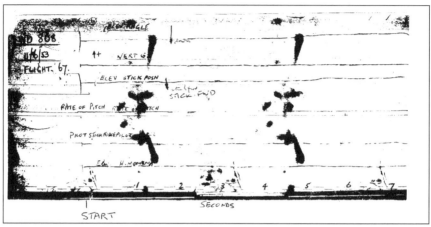

1. Start of test. Note stick forward is downwards on record.

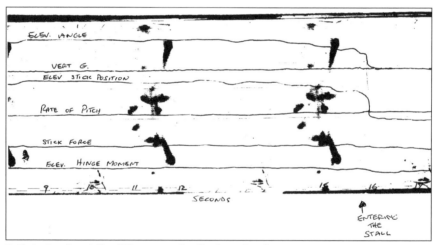

2. Entering the stall at fifteen seconds after lowering flaps.

aircraft during flight manoeuvres. One of the relevant pieces of equipment in this case was a chart recorder which gave traces recording movements of the flying controls, stick (control column) position, etc. (Reproduced above and right). What Peter Lawrence was doing was to explore low speed flying characteristics with aft CG (Centre of Gravity), in accordance with a programme laid down by the aerodynamicists. The test was being conducted at 12,500ft. During the test run, Peter Lawrence selected flaps down, which can be clearly seen in the record.

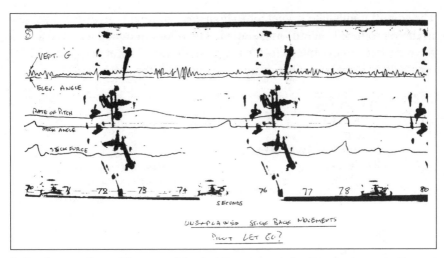

3. On the way down. Note unexplained stick movements backwards at seventy-five and seventy-eight seconds. The pilot had held the stick hard forward throughout the descent in an attempt to get the nose down and recover. Did he let go of the stick at seventy-five and seventy-eight seconds and why? Did he try and eject, couldn't release the canopy? Did he let go of the stick to try and manually force the canopy open? This is about the point where ejection would have been expected.

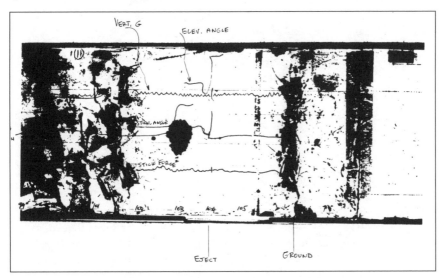

4. Final. Ejection at 104 seconds and ground impact at 106 seconds. Stick let go at 103 seconds, with sudden recorder jump at 104 seconds, probably caused by reaction from seat ejection gun.

The aircraft immediately went into a high nose up condition (also can be seen in the reproduced record) and stalled. The pilot attempted a conventional recovery procedure, but unfortunately the aircraft did not respond and did not recover. He was in what came to be known as the 'deep stall'.

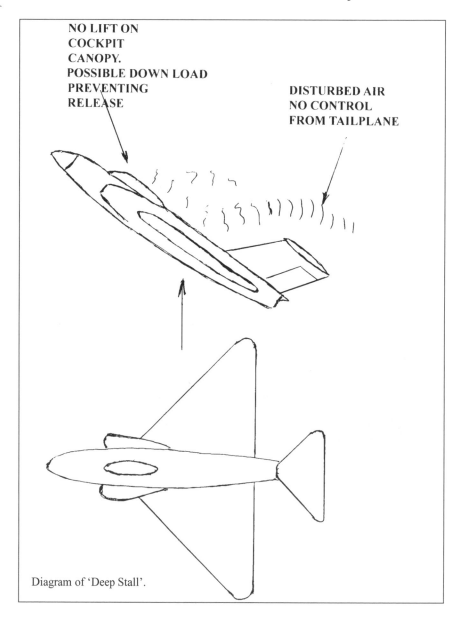

NO LIFT ON COCKPIT CANOPY. POSSIBLE DOWN LOAD PREVENTING RELEASE

DISTURBED AIR NO CONTROL FROM TAILPLANE

Diagram of 'Deep Stall'.

Automatic observer records showed that he tried every combination of throttle setting and control movement, but nothing would change the pitch attitude of the aircraft. It stayed in the stall condition whatever the pilot did, and all the time, of course, losing altitude. The records show that the total time from entering the stall to impact on the ground was a mere ninety seconds, which means that the falling speed was something like 140ft/sec. or 95mph.

He stayed with the aircraft until the last second and then ejected. Sadly, when he ejected, the aircraft was virtually on the ground. He never left the seat. Today we have ejection seats that can be used at ground level, but not at that time. He could have left the aircraft when he first radioed, 'I'm in trouble'. But he didn't – he stayed with the aircraft to try and sort the problem.

The nagging question remains. Why did he leave it too late to eject safely? The theory at the time was that he ejected when his altimeter showed 1,000ft, but didn't realise that he had strayed from being over water to being over ground, at a height of about 1,000ft above sea level. The altimeter would have been set at sea level and, therefore, when reading 1,000ft, he was actually at ground level. But this has never been a very satisfactory explanation. Peter Lawrence was a very experienced pilot and, even in these dramatic circumstances, it has always been something of a mystery that he did not realise where he was and allow for ground height.

But now, some fifty years later, information has come by chance to the author that throws a completely different light on the matter. This will be discussed later.

The other nagging question was why would the aircraft not recover from the stall? Subsequent analysis and investigation would show why. To understand this, it might be helpful for the layman to discuss briefly the conventional stall, shown in the diagram. Any aircraft only stays in the air as a result of forward speed creating lift forces on the wing (apart that is from rotating wing types, helicopters, autogyros, etc). As already mentioned, the lift force is a function of the square of the forward speed and a lift coefficient which depends on the wing section and, of concern to us here, the angle of attack of the wing to the flowing air stream. The lift will increase as the angle of attack increases up to a point. At a critical angle the lift coefficient will suddenly and dramatically reduce. Therefore, for a given set of flight conditions, as speed is reduced the angle of attack is increased to maintain lift and keep the aeroplane in the air. This process can continue to the point where the sudden reduction in lift coefficient takes place – the aircraft has now stalled. So now we have the situation of a high angle of attack, maybe twenty or twenty five degrees, very little forward speed and, suddenly, no lift. The aircraft starts to lose altitude very rapidly.

With a conventional type of fuselage/wing configuration there are established techniques for recovering from a stall condition. Some control is still available to get the nose down or maybe drop a wing and regain some forward speed to restore lift and recover. But not so on the Javelin. With a high angle of attack, little or no forward speed and rapid loss of altitude, the high tail plane is completely blanketed from any wind force that might exist and cannot therefore exert any control. The large wing plan form maintains lateral stability and ailerons are ineffective due to lack of forward speed. The aircraft is now in a stalled and totally stable condition, dropping rapidly towards earth, later to become known as a 'super stall', from which there is no recovery by conventional means. Subsequently, all Javelins were fitted with a tail parachute that could be deployed in the event of an inadvertent stall and which would get the tail up to a position where control could be restored.

It was a tragedy that at a later date the same thing happened to another high tail aircraft, the BAC111 prototype.

To me, an engineer, to whom cause and effect were logical sequences to be explored; to whom determination and exploration of recorded facts and experimental results, along with the recording and publication of events and conclusions, was second nature; this seemed inexplicable. We had suffered a tragedy. It was well known that it was at least partly due to the high tail configuration of the aircraft and the unknown nature of the 'super stall'. How did someone else later come to do the same thing? There would have been a detailed accident investigation report published in due course, with full findings and conclusions, but the immediate reaction at the time was one of horror and shocked disbelief.

The full flight envelope of any prototype aircraft of course has to be explored, including behaviour at the stall; that is what test flying is all about to explore and fully understand all the characteristics of the aircraft and, where necessary, to determine the 'no go' areas that have to be avoided in normal service or commercial operations. Every test flight is planned, every move recorded, analysed and compared with predictions. Conclusions would be recorded, published and discussed. Much liaison would be effected at that time through the Royal Aircraft Establishment at Farnborough, where worked the leading scientists, aerodynamicists, structural engineers and control engineers in the aircraft industry.

To an engineer only in possession of what he had seen and heard it seemed straightforward enough. The knowledge of one accident had not been applied to another situation and there was another accident and someone else died. That is how it appeared at the time; but age and experience shows that the real world is not like that and that there were probably good and sound reasons for what happened, with everyone involved doing their very best with information available. And, of course, this was the time of the Cold War and the Official Secrets Act, sometimes applied rigorously without regard for human situations.

One of the worst things that I had to do during this period was to be forced to discharge a young, enthusiastic and talented engineer, on instructions from above. I was told that, under the Official Secrets Act, he had to go immediately. I will never forget the shock and disbelief of the man concerned. I was not allowed to tell him why. Only that he was to go immediately. His crime? It appeared that his father, a talented and well known musician, had at one time been a member of the communist party. That was all.

One of the great problems in any investigation and the aftermath is different people's perception of the same observed event. The true scientist deals only with recorded and verified facts, with controls built in to eliminate possibilities of mis-observations and random un-connected happenings. Experiments can be repeated over and over again as necessary to determine statistical factors. An accident happens once. Investigations are dependent on observations at the time from instruments. And from witnesses.

At the time of the Javelin accident people were still looking, still stunned by what had happened, still wondering, asking questions and, inevitably, eye witnesses had turned up who said they had seen the whole thing and could help.

One such person that we interviewed said – 'Oh yes, I saw it all. He came down and circled round. He went behind those trees over there and then he came out again and then he tried to land in this field and he crashed.' It was known, of course, that that was impossible. It was quite clear that the aircraft had come straight down out of control. Another said with great authority that he had seen parts fall off the aircraft. With hindsight, might this actually have been the ejector seat that he saw? But that was virtually at zero feet and would eject upwards, not looking like something falling off.

What happens? Do people's minds really see these things? Or is it wishful thinking? Do we see what we want to see? Or what we think others want to know? It raises the whole question of human observation in any situation requiring deduction and conclusion. Experimental work is a long and often tedious series of tests, making observations of results, recording, analysing, coming to a conclusion and formulating the next step. Sometimes we are looking for relatively small effects. We want a result. We have to have an explanation. It seems part of all human nature that we have to be able to explain what we see. The mind cannot grasp that which apparently has no rational explanation, and it seems that sometimes the mind will ignore what is actually there, because it cannot rationalise it; it will present a picture for which there has to be an explanation.

Our witness could not grasp the situation of an aircraft falling vertically out of the sky, rather like a falling leaf. Such things do not happen within his knowledge. Aeroplanes circle, looking for somewhere to land. There is no doubt that this is what his mind saw. It was not as simple as him consciously trying to please by telling us what he thought was wanted. He told the truth as he saw it. This makes human observations very dangerous in some situations. How much is it affected by stress and circumstances at the time? There are many recorded instances of wrong observations and deduction leading to disaster. A classic case is the loss of an aircraft that flew into the ground in poor visibility. Investigation showed that the aircraft instruments were functioning correctly and would have showed the aircraft at ground level, but the crew had other observations that convinced them that the instruments were incorrect and that they had to lose altitude.

How often, one wonders, is our experimental work distorted by our mind altering something it cannot grasp? We could devise experiments to find out. We could run tests, record results, examine what different people see and try and determine what the truth was. But how would we know that what we were observing was the real truth? How do we know, in any experimental work, that what we see and record is not a distortion in our mind of what is actually happening? What is the truth? The use of instruments is, of course, a help. It is said the camera cannot lie – but we still have to interpret what we see. Our mind still has to try and grasp something that perhaps it didn't want to grasp and doesn't understand.

A personal experience of an accident of this sort and its aftermath raises all sorts of doubts. Questions remain unanswered. Do we really know what we are doing? Is what we think happened really what happened? In how many other fields do experts pronounce, come to conclusions, influence decisions, change the future on evidence based on experiments that may be flawed through no fault of any person involved? Simply that observations were what was apparently seen, but which may not be the truth.

In our case, one person may well have known but he did not survive.

Later, it was understood what had happened to the aircraft and why recovery could not be made from the stall. But the question remains unanswered – is this what Peter Lawrence intended to do when he took off on that fateful morning? Was it intended that he should deliberately and almost immediately put the aircraft into that position? The brief for the test flight was to explore the low speed characteristics with aft CG (Centre of Gravity), and the aircraft was loaded accordingly before flight. It had long been gossip that there was a possible problem at low speed that was not explored. It was rumoured that the chief test pilot was concerned and was practising caution, whereas others were becoming impatient.

On the morning in question, there was witness to the fact that there was some degree of tension between Peter Lawrence and the Chief Test Pilot, Bill Waterton. What it was about is, of course, unknown, but there is no doubt that, for whatever reason, Peter Lawrence was not in the best of tempers when he took off and started the flight. Did this affect his actions?

The witnessing of the incident that might have contributed to some tension took place from a point of vantage high up in the hangar where the Chief Test Pilot's office was located. Testing was in progress on some of the flying controls of a Javelin. I was looking at the tail and rudder controls from a staging high up by the tail plane and the Chief Test Pilot's office door was in full view.

It seemed that something was amiss when the door flew open and words were heard. Peter Lawrence appeared in the doorway and appeared to be flinging words over his shoulder as he left. He appeared to be upset about something. He was then seen to go immediately to WD808 and take off for the ill-fated flight.

It may well have been a normal pre-flight discussion and, no doubt, there is always some tension. After all, test flying is a dangerous job. I have seen F1 drivers before a race showing irritation and temper and no doubt the same thing happens in test flying. But did it affect judgement? It leaves the nagging question that haunts memories. Did it affect what happened on the flight? All test flying is dangerous and carries risks, by its very nature, but was the risk inflamed by the apparent pre-flight tension?

Peter Lawrence was carrying out simulated approaches at low speed close to, or at, the stall with the aircraft rigged with aft CG. The objective was to investigate elevator response under these conditions. The records show that initially flaps were up, and then selected down. At this point the aircraft immediately entered a high nose up attitude, recorded as being up to fifty degrees, and then came down out of control. The record shows the control column being pushed fully forward, elevators down, in an attempt to correct the nose up change of trim. But the aircraft remained in the 'super stall' condition. Nothing that the pilot did appeared to make any difference. Not that there was much time – total time from initiation of the stall to impact is recorded as ninety seconds.

Questions remain. Was this the flight test that was intended at this time? Was it planned to be Peter Lawrence's flight? How much was already known about the behaviour of the aircraft at low speed? The answers will never be known. Many records were destroyed or lost after the closure of Gloster Aircraft Co. in 1960. Many people are no longer with us. For some of us still here the tragedy of that flight will live in memory for ever.

It must be remembered however, that this took place over fifty years ago, in 1953. These are the recollections of a young engineer given, at an early age, responsibility for the testing and development of the flying controls and other systems on the aircraft, but not privy to many other aspects, although often attending co–ordinating meetings and investigative meetings after the accident. There were many other very clever people in senior positions who would probably have known more of the circumstances. The aerodynamicists, stress engineers, flight development managers, designers. The whole team that exists to develop a prototype aeroplane into the efficient fighting machine intended by the operational specification that initiated the design.

Recollections that have been nursed for all this time with unanswered questions. Should it have happened? Should the BAC accident have happened? Cameo pictures as clear in the mind now as when seen fifty years ago. The aircraft in a corner of a field, flat on the ground, crumpled but intact. The burnt out centre section. The acrid smell still hanging in the air. The blades of grass; not even bent, incredibly growing straight up behind the wing trailing edge. The group of people, sombre, distressed, but already minds working, wondering, planning, finding out, so it doesn't happen again. Retrieving the records. The records that will provide information on what actually happened in terms of physical dimensions, in terms of things that can be measured by instruments. But that is all. They do not, and can not, tell what went on in people's minds. They tell part of the truth, but not all.

And, a little apart from the wreckage and the people, that small piece of what was humanity. That reminder of the frailty of life. The only record that would really have known the answer. That does know the answer.

The answer to the one great mystery. Why did he leave it so late to eject?

As mentioned earlier, it was generally assumed that Peter Lawrence was so busy with the aircraft after the stall, that he did not realise he was over high ground. The theory was that he ejected when he thought he had about 1,000ft left under him, when, in fact, he was virtually at ground level. It has always been difficult to accept that theory. Peter Lawrence was a very experienced pilot and it seemed unlikely that he did not know where he was and that he would not know he was over high ground when he ejected. As we have seen, he did make a heroic effort to recover from the stall and stayed with the aircraft when he could have ejected much earlier.

But it was still something of a mystery – just why did he leave it so late? Questions, questions unanswered and memories. Memories of all the years, the struggles, the triumphs and the failures that keep coming back. And now, just recently, some fifty years after the event, by an incredible coincidence, a possible solution has come to light. Now put forward for the first time after all these years in the page following

A Possible Solution
A letter was published in the September 2000 issue of the Royal Aeronautical Society Journal, Aerospace, which prompted a reply from the author which was published in the November issue.

This prompted another letter from a correspondent published in the December issue. This is of great importance. This correspondent reveals that prior to the Peter Lawrence tragedy, there had been no wind tunnel tests at high angles of attack. Worse than that, this piece of information was deleted by a security officer at the Ministry of Supply from an article prepared by the correspondent that would have revealed the truth. The truth was that, initially, no wind tunnel tests had been carried out at angles of attack above twenty-five degrees.

Of even more significance is a hand written letter received privately by the author. This was from someone actually working on wind tunnel tests subsequent to the accident. A relevant extract from the letter is re-produced here.

ON THE EDGE OF FLIGHT

"...Those heroic days"

I read with great interest the letter from Brian Brinkworth (September *Aerospace International*) concerning the Gloster Javelin in the 1950s and, in his words, "...those heroic days." His letter has stirred up many memories of those days and my time in the Research Department at Gloster working for the chief research engineer at the time (Geoff Longford, a brilliant and dedicated engineer from whom I learnt much) on the development of the aircraft systems and powered flying controls in particular. I finished up as chief of engineering research when Geoff Longford became chief of flight test engineering before the defence contract cancellations brought it all to a close with the loss of so much progress in technology.

I focus in particular on the incident in which Bill Waterton force landed WD804 at Boscombe Down. What happened was divergent elevator flutter, resulting in the total loss of elevators. Trim was accomplished at that time by an all moving tailplane driven by an electric actuator. Waterton succeeded in controlling the aircraft by trim in level flight but lost it on landing. As the 'controls man' I was generally rushed to the scene of the several Javelin accidents that we later unfortunately experienced, but this was the first and the scene remains strong in my memory. Flight recorders were, of course, in operation and records were retrieved.

It was, as Brian Brinkworth says, a fine piece of airmanship, but it should not overshadow the courage and dedication of others at Gloster in those days, some of whom unfortunately lost their lives. I think especially of Peter Lawrence. He was a man much admired and liked who lost his life when exploring the stall with aft CG in prototype WD808. He entered what became known as the 'super stall' from which he could not recover, due to the high tailplane being blanketed by the delta wing. He stayed with the aircraft, trying various combinations of stall recovery techniques and finally ejected. Unfortunately, he had drifted over high ground and died in his seat. Again, I was at the scene shortly after the accident and I still have a copy of one of the flight recordings, from the start to the end.

I think of others who displayed supreme airmanship in other circumstances, among them 'Dicky' Martin, who later became chief test pilot. Jan Zurawkowski with his superb 'cartwheel' manoeuvre at Farnborough. Geoff Worral who took off a production aircraft and found that the trim control had reverse polarity, but managed to sort it out. Brian Smith, who lost his life in a collision accident, and Flt Lt J. Ross who lost his life after losing control of a Javelin over the Bristol Channel. I remember also the Boscombe Down test pilot who successfully landed a Javelin after losing powered aileron control in what was a fully powered but duplicated system with no manual reversion, a feat that seemed almost impossible at the time. I spent some weeks at Boscombe finding out what went wrong. That, and the sequel, is a story in itself.

There is much more, reaching back to the Meteor, also with much drama attached, for which there is not space in a letter, but I feel it so important that these memories should not be lost; they are part of our aviation history and the years of endeavour.

Eric Absolon, MRAeS

Figs. 7: Letter from author published in *Aerospace*.

Javelin security

The letter from Eric Absolon (November *Aerospace International*) reminded me of what I learned when researching a description of Javelin development which appeared in *The Aeroplane* for 14 November 1958.

With regard to the accident which cost Peter Lawrence his life, this article was edited to read (p 722) "...Investigation of stalling behaviour at the RAE with wind-tunnel models had been limited to an angle-of-attack well above the normal stall, but from further investigation at higher angles there emerged the 'super stall' phenomenon." That was true, but it wasn't the whole story.

In light of the Lawrence tragedy on 11 June 1953, I had enquired about model testing and learned to my amazement that there had been NO initial tunnel testing at angles of attack above 25°. However, that revelation was cut out of the draft by the security officer at the Ministry of Supply to whom the article had to be submitted more than five years later when the Javelin FAW8 was declassified. As is so often the case, 'security' was really not military but that of the officials concerned.

It would make an interesting research study of aircraft development to determine how much has been lost by overzealous 'security' as opposed to how much might have been gained by its absence. When working on a US Navy VSX (S-3A) bid proposal at Lockheed in the late 1960s, I was shown a heavily classified Navy document with a section headed 'The Real Threat'. To my astonishment, this threat turned out to be not Russia or China but the US Air Force because of the fight for funding.

On another occasion, I was loaned to Vought with a colleague to produce a 48-page executive summary of the VFX (F-14A) bid proposal but, on arrival in Texas, was detained on instructions from security. It transpired that Lockheed security was worried that Vought security would be worried that I was a British-born Canadian citizen, albeit with a US security clearance. The Vought vice-president in charge of the proposal quickly disabused Lockheed of the notion, but we lost half a day out of the 13 remaining before the submission deadline. The second week we set a new record for Lockheed by working 129 hours.

There must be many others who have had similar experiences of "security" being used to cover ineptitude.

David Godfrey, MRAeS

Reply to letter published in *Aerospace*. December 2000

THE LOSS OF PETER LAWRENCE

I was working in the low speed tunnels at RAE Farnborough. One of my jobs was to investigate the loads on the canopy in the super stall. The tests were done in the 24ft tunnel using a fairly large model of the Javelin cockpit, seat and pilot all dynamically sealed and the canopy was mounted on a strain gauge balance. At that time air loads on the canopy were assumed to be sufficient to remove it, but we found from the tunnel tests that there were very small upward loads on the canopy and that the pilot would be unable to push it open.

In the light of this dramatic information, the records taken from the aircraft were re-examined. They indicate, quite clearly, a point where Peter Lawrence let go of the controls some two seconds before impact. The control column that had been held fully forward in a recovery attempt is released and moves back. Clearly, this is when he attempted to eject. At that point he would have had about 200ft of altitude. It is believed that, in fact, the seat had hardly left the aircraft until ground level. Remember that the aircraft was falling downwards at something like 120ft/sec, so the relative seat velocity upwards would have been very small. Remember also that this was before the development of ground level ejection seats.

But, looking back through the record, there are other unexplained control column movements. See photograph, 'On the way down'. This is about thirty seconds from impact and shows several control column movements backwards at about three second intervals. Why? Why would Peter Lawrence do this when he was holding the stick hard forward in an attempt to get the nose down and recover? Was it because he had released the canopy in preparation for ejection, but it wouldn't go? Was he trying desperately to push off the canopy so that he could eject, and had to let go of the control column momentarily?

It seems entirely possible now, in the light of the Farnborough wind tunnel tests, that he released the canopy, but it did not leave the aircraft. He had to struggle to push the canopy off manually. That may have cost him his life.

The information from Farnborough was transmitted to the company at some point and a pneumatic system of canopy ejection was developed. But memory is that this was not fitted until later in prototype development. If it had been applied, how do we explain the delay in ejection?

Why were wind tunnel tests at high angles of attack not carried out before the tragedy?

And why was the BAC111 lost under similar 'super stall' conditions almost a year later?

Lack of communication? The Official Secrets Act? We shall probably never know.

So many questions, so many memories.

The memories – the memories of a lifetime of dreaming about aeroplanes and the privilege of working with aeroplanes.

Chapter 2

How It All Began

When did I first start to think about aeroplanes? I don't know, but I suppose it all began seventy-nine years ago when I was coming up to my seventh birthday. My brother and I used to roam the fields quite freely and, after one such happy day – must have been in early September, I don't remember school getting in the way – went to bed tired and happy. But with hindsight probably feeling slightly off colour after having feasted on blackberries in the fields. Something that we did – just went out there in the fields and woods. Roamed around, not afraid of anything, no fears or worries. Ate blackberries and something else. We dug them out of the ground, recognised by the green tops. A kind of root or tuber, very tasty.

Anyway, the next day dawned. I woke up in the morning and went to get out of bed and run around as usual. But it didn't work. I got out of bed, but then fell flat on the floor. My legs wouldn't work. I couldn't walk and I remember the great feeling of not understanding. What had happened? I couldn't walk. I couldn't get up. And I felt so sick. Everything became rather vague and confusing. I don't remember much else for a while. But I remember the doctor coming. And I remember being so sure of what had happened.

'I know, I said, I know what's wrong, I know why I feel so sick. Yesterday I ate too many blackberries.'

'Oh yes, said the doctor, and how many would that be?'

'I ate 147 blackberries,' I said. 'That's what done it. I ate 147 blackberries and now I'm sick.'

What it actually was, of course, was polio. Commonly known as Infantile Paralysis in those days. But that wouldn't have been known at first. The doctor may have suspected, but it was off to hospital. I often think about my mother at that time. Of any mother in that situation. My father probably at

21

work, and here was this doctor telling my mother that her eldest son was sick, very sick. Paralysed. And the ambulance coming to take him away to hospital. And she was left with the younger son to look after. Did she come to the hospital? I have no idea. Did the neighbours help? I have no idea. My grandparents were living with us at the time, I think. Or did they come later? I have no memory.

All I remember so vividly is being in hospital. In hospital for my birthday. In hospital for Christmas. In hospital for six long months, lying in bed, unable to get up or walk. What did I do all day? What were they doing to me? With hindsight, what treatment was I receiving, if any? I do remember, right at the beginning, must have been not long after arriving, a bunch of nurses around my cot (yes, I was put in a cot to start with, not a bed) trying to stop a deformity setting in. The nurses very prim and proper, with their pristine uniforms. White caps stiffly starched.

My right foot was going out straight and there was nothing I could do to stop it. The nurses wound rolls of plaster round my foot and strapped it back to my knee in a vain effort to stop the foot from straightening out. Even as a child, I remember thinking at the time how silly that was. Nothing was going to stop this deformity.

Sometime later I was transferred to a men's ward and there I stayed. What did I do? I really don't remember much. I don't remember visitors, but there must have been visitors. Of course, in those days, visiting was strictly limited to controlled visiting hours. But surely my mother and father must have come? But I have no recollection of that. I do remember my grandmother coming in and bringing me a bible. I started to read at Genesis 1 and just read every word. I don't know how far I got. And the men used to get newspapers. Sometimes they would let me have one when they had finished with it. I remember so clearly, I used to start at the top of page one and just read every word on every page. I imagine the stories didn't make any sense to me, but it was something to do, just to pass the time. But pass the time to what? There was no tomorrow, nothing to look forward to, no feeling of perhaps going home at some time. I don't remember any feeling of progress, any feeling of getting better, no change in anything, just lying there.

Looking back now, that seems so unfair on my parents. They must have been worried and sad and they had their own problems. I don't think my mother was very well and my father was struggling to earn a living driving a petrol tanker, doing something he must have hated so much after having to give up his farm in his beloved Norfolk.

HOW IT ALL BEGAN

In those days people died in hospital. Well, they still do I suppose from time to time. But in that ward it seemed to happen all the time. The bodies seemed to be left during the day and moved out at night. Or was it that people died at night time? Screens were put up all down the ward. We were supposed to be asleep and not know what was going on. But, of course, a small boy that couldn't sleep much anyway was curious and awake. By twisting around in my bed I could glimpse what was going on and see the body being taken away. Another one gone. Did it affect me? I don't know. I suppose it must have done, otherwise I wouldn't have such vivid memories, some of it as though it was yesterday instead of over eighty years ago. If anything, it probably gave me a determination to move on. Except that I couldn't, not then anyway because I couldn't walk, I couldn't even get out of bed.

Not that I would criticise the nurses or doctors. They were doing their best with what was available at that time. Knowledge and technology was limited compared to today. Sometimes, perhaps, we should stand back and marvel at what has been achieved in a lifetime instead of being so quick to criticise the apparent faults and shortcomings in the NHS. It's truly amazing what has happened in one lifetime. At that time epidemics were rife and there wasn't much treatment. Children got sick with diphtheria, scarlet fever, smallpox and many died. I remember later, at Southampton, seeing children running around in the streets with no shoes or socks and very little clothing, often sick, flushed with fever. And there was very little help. There was some form of medical insurance, I imagine by one of the insurance companies. Sixpence a week was collected and that provided some basic doctor's attendance. My father's wages at that time were probably about £3/week. I don't know what happened about hospital costs.

But, during that time, perhaps something began to emerge in me. Perhaps it was the thought of freedom, the freedom to move around, the freedom to go anywhere, not to be dependent on the body and legs. The freedom to fly like a bird. The freedom not to be limited, the freedom not to be restricted by a body that didn't work properly. The freedom to forget all of that and think about the sky and the clouds, the unlimited space.

Perhaps that was when I first started to think about aeroplanes. Commercial aviation was of course in its infancy, but great strides had been made in the twelve or thirteen years since the end of the First World War and it was not uncommon to see an aircraft in the sky to stir the imagination and set the pulse racing at the thought of soaring like a bird. The Wright

Brothers' first flight was in 1908 (over 100 years ago as I write). Just six years after that the First World War started and that created the urge to get into the air. Perfect for observation of enemy movements and so on. All the sordid business of how to inflict the heaviest casualties on the enemy, how to destroy the enemy army, how to destroy the most people. First of all done with balloons. They could hover almost stationary, or even be tethered to the ground and allowed to drift over enemy positions. But, of course, that led to the development of the means of destroying the balloons. The new ability of powered flight, as demonstrated by the Wright Bros. was the perfect answer. And so great strides in aviation were made during the four long years of war, sadly at the expense of so many lives.

Anyway, back to the hospital. Eventually, somebody decided it was time to get me up. On what basis and why it took so long, I have no idea. Perhaps there was treatment I don't remember, or perhaps the disease just took its course and that's how long it took. Whatever the reason, one day, some six months after admission, the nurses came along in their beautifully starched and ironed blue and white uniforms and said, 'Come on, we're going to get you up.' So they did. They stood me on my feet, holding on tight, and encouraged me to try and take a step. One leg slowly moves in front of the other. 'That's good, now the other one.' And so on and so on. This went on and on. Each day a little more movement. And then, one day, the miracle. I took some steps on my own. Eventually I was able to walk a little way and then the magic words! You're going home!

I don't remember the going, or the arriving at home. All I remember is that suddenly, there I was back at home. But it wasn't as simple as that. There was school to think about. And it turned out I had to go to outpatients at the hospital three times a week for sunray treatment and massage to help in getting things going again. And, for some reason that I have never understood to this day, a doctor would spend what seemed like ages looking at my finger nails. Must have been looking for something, but what?

However, I must have managed to get to school, although it meant walking; there was no other way. I do remember later walking to the primary school. It seemed a long way then for me, but probably not far in reality. Just down the road, over the bridge, round a side street and there it was. Three or four classrooms and in memory, probably faulty, a corrugated iron roof. There was a playground and some basic toilets across from that. Milk was provided for every child. It came in one third of a pint bottles, specially produced for schools. Someone in government must have decreed that every child must have milk. Central concern for the health of the nation. So what's new?

I do remember that the teachers were wonderful. Totally dedicated. They must have done a good job for one small boy who, perforce, was not at school as much as he should have been and yet managed to acquire the basics of an education. Those years at primary school must surely be some of the most formative years of our short life here on this planet.

Going to outpatients at the hospital was quite a problem all that time. Sometimes a neighbour used to take me and sometimes my grandfather, who was living with us at the time. We had to go on the tram and then, I suppose, walk from the tram stop to the hospital. Coming home the tram lines came to an end just short of the bridge over the River Itchen and I think we must have got off the tram there and caught a bus. I remember on one occasion my grandfather telling me to wait while he jumped off the tram while it was still moving – I suppose to catch the bus and ask the driver to wait. But I wasn't going to wait and tried to jump off after him. Of course, I fell in the road and I have memories still of a confusion of lights and cars with me lying in the road. Health and Safety rules and regulations didn't exist then; everybody took care of themselves.

But, during this time, with not much schooling and long periods of inactivity I began to dream. To dream about flying like a bird, to soar in the sky and leave all earthly problems behind. My father at that time had had to take whatever work he could and was driving a fuel tanker for what was then known as Shell Mex and BP. Now two separate companies, Shell International and BP. He must have detested what he had to do. I still remember the smell of petrol on his clothes when he came home worn out.

He did, however, have some interesting duties and sometimes he would take me with him, in the cab of the tanker. One of his rounds was to take aviation fuel to the airport at Eastleigh and he took me with him one day to see this wonderful new aeroplane that had just been produced by Supermarine. The Supermarine works were nearby at Woolston, on the River Itchen. It was there that they produced the Schneider Trophy aircraft that were so successful.

This wonderful new aeroplane had its pedigree in the successful range of Schneider Trophy aircraft. It was painted blue and had a two bladed wooden propeller. It was, of course, the prototype Spitfire, registered as K5054 the very first Spitfire that later became so famous in the Second

World War. And I saw it fly. That really set me alight, fired my imagination and set me dreaming of what I wanted to do. (see photograph in plates)

There were others. Two German seaplanes used to come in to Southampton Water to refuel and my father took fuel to them. They would taxi in to Woolston and my father used to go out in a boat with barrels of fuel. The larger, from memory, was the Dornier DoX. A relatively large aircraft with six engines and, I think, with two propellers per engine, one behind as a pusher. (see photograph in plates)

The other was a smaller aircraft, a Junkers Ju-46, that was carried on the ship '*Bremen*' and catapulted off to deliver mail at Southampton and refuel. The pressure to carry and deliver more in shorter times was beginning to take effect. It would drive progress in aviation, both technically and commercially up to the outbreak of war, when everything took on a new dimension.

Another memory is that of the 'piggy back' aircraft the Short-Mayo 'Mercury-Maia' Composite. (see photograph) You don't hear much about that now, but it was all part of the drive to carry more load, more passengers, further and faster. All part of the developing civilian aircraft business. All aircraft have to get off the ground before they can be in their element and perform the job that they are designed to do. Taxiing on the runway and the take-off run to get sufficient speed to become airborne consume a disproportionate amount of fuel. Fuel that has to be carried at the expense of payload; and it is only payload that will make the aircraft commercially viable. So, someone had the idea of carrying a small aircraft on the back of a larger aircraft just to get off the ground. A 'piggy back' aircraft. Once the combination was airborne and at sufficient altitude, the smaller aircraft was released and flew off on its own. That way, the smaller, commercial aircraft did not have to carry fuel for take-off and its payload and range were increased. In theory this made it more commercially viable, but in practice it didn't survive. I imagine the technical and engineering problems were massive at that time. Also, already, the shadow of war was looming and people's minds were turning to other things.

During this time, my polio leg was quite badly deformed and walking was not easy. I suppose I stood out as being different at school and children can be cruel, probably without realising the hurt they can cause. They used to jump on my back and pull me down and then I would have a struggle to get up again. But all done I suppose in fun. And then, when I was around 10 years old, my parents came to hear, through a truly dedicated and caring family doctor, of a wonderful hospital – Lord Mayor Treloars Hospital for Cripples.

The hospital was at Alton, about 30 miles from Southampton were they ran a clinic. So, I was taken to the clinic and there examined by a truly remarkable orthopaedic surgeon, Mr Langston. He checked everything, got me to walk up and down the room and finally my parents were told, yes, we could do something for him, but it will mean some surgery and a few stays in the hospital.

But here was a problem. What about the cost? The hospital was founded by Lord Mayor Treloar of London with a Trust. But obviously there were running costs involved. Patients had to be kept, nurses and staff paid, doctors and surgeons paid, although it would not surprise me to know that they gave much of their time for free. Everybody there was totally dedicated to making twisted bodies whole – getting children to walk again who were otherwise denied.

So, what about the cost to parents of the children being treated? Well, as I understand it, parents were asked how much they thought they could afford towards maintenance and that was what they paid. No further questions, no checking, no investigations; just based on trust. Certainly my parents could not have afforded very much. A petrol tanker driver was not exactly overpaid. One cannot help making comparisons with today. What have we lost in this modern world?

So, they took me into the hospital at Alton. I remember so clearly, my mother took me to the clinic at Southampton and from there an ambulance took me to the hospital, on my own. I have this vivid recollection of being in the ambulance at the Southampton clinic and looking out at my mother through the open doors. And then my mother said, 'Well, goodbye then.' That was it, then the doors were closed and I was on my own.

No hug, no anything, just 'goodbye' and there I was, going to a strange place 30 miles away. And I was going to be there for five long months.

I think my mother was finding it very difficult and she did not want to show emotion or get upset. My father, of course, had to be at work. It must have been difficult for them, to see their eldest son crippled and then taken away to somewhere very difficult for them to visit. But they would have known it was for the best in the long run. They wanted me to have the best possible chance.

Going into the hospital was an experience in itself. Admission was first of all in an isolation block. A number of individual rooms, one patient per room, completely isolated – no visitors of course, the same nurse to look after one patient. All boys in the block; girls were quite separate, this was long before the advent of mixed wards. Maximum admission age for boys was sixteen, I think, and the nurses started at the same age. They were totally dedicated. I remember one of the times in isolation a nurse who was determined to polish up a tarnished brass plaque over the bed. A little bit each day, until, eventually it shone like new. She was so proud.

The purpose of isolation, of course, was to prevent disease being taken into the hospital from outside and it seemed to work. I had three stays in Alton altogether (another of four months and then another of three months) and I don't remember one single case of an illness brought in from outside.

After two weeks in isolation and detailed examination by a surgeon, we were prepared for surgery and eventually wheeled down to the operating theatre. The very worst part of the whole experience was the anaesthetic. The first time I was there this consisted of spraying ether on to a kind of mask held over the face. It created a most awful choking sensation and was altogether most unpleasant. I think in later operations a gas was used first, but still unpleasant. In fact, being 'put under' was probably by far the most unpleasant part of my stays in hospital. And that memory has stayed with me to this day. I have not had to undergo an operation since Treloar's, over seventy years ago. The very thought now fills me with dread and I would resist to the utmost. But, I can hear someone asking, what if an operation would relieve you of pain? A knee replacement for example? The answer is, I don't know. I suppose it would depend on how bad the pain and incapacity was. At the moment, I am just grateful that the question hasn't arisen.

Back to Treloar's, after the operation, recovery was back in the isolation ward. I remember coming round after my first operation and the shock of seeing my leg plastered, with the plaster stained with my blood that had seeped through. However, spirits quickly revived, plaster changed, feeling fit and well, but confined to bed. Except on the last visit some four years later. A relatively simple operation to straighten a badly deformed big toe. Simple enough, but the plaster somehow pressed hard on a nerve at the side of my foot and caused the most enormous pain. I was really in trouble. They didn't want to release the plaster in case it upset the orthopaedic work that had been done, but they did their best and eventually cut a small piece out at the side that gave some relief. So it had to stay until, I suppose, the toe was partly set and the plaster could be changed.

Once all this was done and a new plaster fitted, it was just a case of waiting for twelve to fourteen weeks for everything to fully set and it was possible to put weight on the leg. So, after probably four weeks in isolation, transfer to one of the main wards took place and there you stayed in bed until it was time to have the plaster removed, get up and learn to walk – again! These days, a steel hoop would be fitted at the bottom of the plaster and walking could continue. But not then. I imagine that the surgeons were just not prepared to take the risk of their good work being undone. After all, it was pioneering surgery. Without that, nothing would have been done and I (and many others) would have continued as a cripple.

Over my three stays I first had what was known, from memory, as a 'Dunn's arthridisis', to straighten the ankle joint and fix it so that my foot was more or less pointing in the direction of walking. But it is fixed, with only limited swivelling movement. This was followed by a 'Subcutaneous elongation of the tendon Achilles' (SETA). This means lengthening the Achilles tendon at the back of the ankle, which, as part of the deformity of the polio, had tightened up so that my foot was permanently pointing downwards, so that I walked on my toes on the affected foot. This was a particularly clever piece of surgery at that time. The whole operation was performed through two tiny incisions in the back of the ankle that healed without any scar whatsoever.

And finally, the straightening of the badly deformed big toe. That doesn't sound very much, but it was amazing the difference that it made to walking and comfort. I could wear normal shoes again. In fact, it is difficult to exaggerate the incredible difference that those three visits to Treloars made to my life. I learnt to walk normally and few people that didn't know me had any idea of my problem.

After the surgery, we were moved out of isolation on to one of the wards. The hospital was arranged in five blocks in an arc, all on one floor, with two wards to each block. Girls and boys were well separated! There was a complete mixture of different levels of illness and disability. Some, like me, no longer ill and just waiting for healing after the surgery. Others still suffering one way or another. I remember one boy who had to have more surgery. TB and osteomylitis were rife and required continual attention. This boy came back from surgery and later he was taken in to a side passage to remove and change his dressing. Suddenly there were screams of anguish that went on and on. They had had to amputate his leg and he didn't know until the dressing was removed.

But life went on and boys were boys, getting up to all sorts of things.

Discipline was strong – I suppose it had to be. There were Matron's rounds at 9.00am. Everything had to be neat and tidy and spotlessly clean. In the afternoon there was school. Yes, school. Governesses came round to the bedside and gave us instructions and work to do. It was to a very high standard. But in between it was up to us. Stamp collecting was a big thing. My stamp collection is still around somewhere. Something called 'Approval sheets' came from dealers and you could pick stamps that you wanted (and could afford from pocket money) and then send the money to the dealers. I don't know what they did if somebody didn't pay.

One of my spells there was not long before having to take what was known as the Scholarship, to get in to secondary school. I went from hospital almost straight to the examination. I passed. That can only have been due to the exceptional skill and dedication of the governesses at Treloar's. I remember well being put up on the platform in front of the whole assembled school as an example of what can be done. Embarrassing!

One of the more memorable experiences at Alton was, on one of my visits, being sent to a branch of the hospital at Hayling Island in Hampshire for convalescence – the long period of waiting for things to heal after the operation, before plaster could be removed. That was a wonderful experience. It was during the summer and all day long beds were pushed outside onto a balcony that extended right out over a beach. I remember on one occasion seeing dolphins and watching them for ages as they dived and surfaced, making those curved appearances above the water. I remember my parents coming to see me while there. It was not so far from Southampton as Alton and I suppose they could manage that. They went to Portsmouth and got the ferry across to Hayling Island. Unfortunately, it was pouring with rain and they walked the whole way, in the rain, from the ferry on the western tip of the island to the hospital which was on the extreme eastern tip of the island, a distance of almost 5 miles. It's hard to imagine the state they must have been in. We complain today about many things, including transport. Perhaps we should remember how hard it was for people just sixty/seventy years ago.

I went back to Hayling Island a few years ago and went to the end of the island where I remembered the hospital. It was gone. Where there had been this wonderful place of recovery, of hope, with memories of dedicated nurses, there was rough area of grass and sand dunes. Nothing left. Nothing to show what an incredible place this had been. I was moved to write an article for the local press and, as I said in that piece of writing, there should be a notice:

This is where miracles were performed, where crippled, twisted bodies were made whole. Treat it with respect.

I did actually return there very recently. 2008 was the centenary of the foundation of Treloar's hospital and special celebrations were held at Alton, commencing with the laying of a wreath on the statue of Lord Mayor Treloar at the old hospital site. The original hospital buildings have long since gone and have been replaced by a new NHS hospital. But the statue to Lord Mayor Treloar is still there in the grounds. The wreath was laid by the granddaughter of Sir Henry Guavain, who pioneered the surgery work undertaken. I was one of only two old patients that were there and it was an emotional and very moving occasion. While there the opportunity was taken to re-visit the site at Hayling Island. It looked as though it was planned for housing development. The end of a chapter.

Did I dream about aeroplanes while I was there? Yes, I suppose I did. I was always dreaming.

In between my spells at hospital, I got into the habit of cycling out to Hamble, about 6 miles from where we lived, to the airfield there. There was an organisation called Air Service Training that trained pilots, I believe right through to full qualification with a view to becoming civil airliner crew. The aircraft were Avro Cadets and Avro Tutors. (see photograph in plates)

I used to go into the airfield through a side gate from the road, leave my bicycle against the hedge and just sit there and watch the flying. I used to dream and wish that I could be a part of it. I used to wander around towards the hangars, looking at the aeroplanes. Anything just to be close and feel a part of it all. I became known to the mechanics and they used to talk to me and, I suppose, offered encouragement to this rather strange and lonely young boy with the gammy leg.

In the hangar there were other aircraft, including a small, high wing type known as the Aeronca JAP, I think. The JAP probably because of a JAP engine, a small, lightweight but powerful engine, used on performance motorcycles of the day. One of the mechanics that took a particular interest in me said that he knew the pilot/owner of this aeroplane and, if I wanted, he could speak to him and arrange for a flight. Did I just! I was so excited and dreamt about it. It was arranged for a certain weekend. I cycled out to Hamble on the appointed day, full of excitement and anticipation. Alas, it was not to be. When I got there, the friendly mechanic had to tell me that it had fallen through, the owner/pilot had changed his mind and could not take me up. With hindsight, I think probably because of insurance complications, or maybe the owner was just too busy or it could have been any one of all sorts of reasons why. One very disappointed boy!

But it didn't put me off in any way – just made me all the more interested and determined. One way or the other I was going to get into aeroplanes! I continued cycling out to Hamble as often as possible and saw all sorts of interesting aircraft. One in particular made a lasting impression. This was a Cierva Autogyro. (see photograph in plates)

I have no idea who it belonged to or why it was at Hamble, but I did see it take off now and then. Even then, although at that time I had not yet learnt anything of the theory of aerodynamics or aircraft design (that came much later) I remember being fascinated by this thing with a propeller on the front and a rotating wing.

For those that don't know, the autogyro is not a helicopter. It is quite different in concept. It has a conventional propeller which propels the aircraft forwards. The forward movement causes the free rotating wing to rotate, which, in turn, generates lift. The end result is an aircraft with short take-off and high manoeuvrability. There have been one or two attempts more recently to resurrect the idea, but it has never really looked like being a viable commercial proposition.

There were many ideas floating around for new developments in aviation at that time. All part of the eternal quest for more speed, more range, more carrying capacity. Some driven by military considerations, some by civil airline needs. But the basic drive was the same – the ability to carry more load further and faster, whether to transport passengers to parts of the world hitherto not available to ordinary people, or weapons of destruction of innocent people caught up in a war of ideology. And sometimes, of course, to prevent an aggressor from pursuing national interests, that would harm nations and innocent people caught up in the aggressors' pursuit of domination. As was the case in the pending war that was looming on the horizon. Little did we know that nothing would ever be the same again.

One such new idea was the Cunliffe Owen 'Flying Wing'. This was proposed as a design, but, as far as I know was never built. The idea was to create a massive wing that could house engines and passenger and/or cargo load within the wing structure. The aerodynamic advantage of such an arrangement is, of course, an efficient lift surface without the drag associated with a conventional fuselage and engine pods mounted on the wing. The difficulty was the massive structural problems that resulted in such a layout. And, not the least, the realisation that for civil use, passengers would not have conventional windows so that they could look out. It could be argued that when flying at high altitude or at night, there is nothing to see anyway. But it was also argued, quite correctly, that passengers would not take kindly to such an arrangement.

For whatever reason, it was a project that did not materialise, although it is interesting to note that similar designs have recently been proposed.

Returning to Hamble, the other excitement there was a flying display day. There were aerobatic displays and a display of low and high altitude bombing using flour bags against a ground target. There was also a dare-devil display of picking up a cloth from the ground using a hook on the wing tip. I cycled out there and spent the day watching. It resolved me that whatever else I did (and who knows what awaited me, I really had no idea) I was going to get into aeroplanes, one way or the other.

There was also the famous Alan Cobham's Flying Circus. This was at Eastleigh Airport and my father took me there to watch. Incredible displays of aerobatics, target bombing and almost unbelievable displays of 'wing walking' – ladies standing on the wing (securely strapped on of course), while the pilot indulged in aerobatics and low flying. So many experiences that continued to fuel my dreams and imagination.

It must have been around this time that I finally realised that I was not going to be an Air Force pilot. I had long nursed the ambition to join the RAF. If I was ever asked what I was going to do when I grew up, the answer was to be a pilot. For a long time I couldn't understand why my father used to try and discourage me and used to suggest that I should, perhaps, think about the civil service. Eventually, I suppose I realised the truth – the truth that I would not be able to join the RAF because of disability. 'But what about Douglas Bader?' I hear someone say. 'He was a pilot and he had no legs.'

Yes, but he was a pilot first. He lost his legs later and was allowed to keep flying. As we all know, he went on to become a hero and a legend of the Second World War. A prime example of how to overcome and not be defeated by circumstances beyond our control.

And then it happened again. A sudden illness, no warning, except that I started to wander in my mind. Started babbling all sorts of nonsense. I became delirious, didn't know what was going on. Again, the call to the doctor. At that time we had a lady doctor, who was quite wonderful and quickly diagnosed pneumonia, in those days quite serious. But the family doctor knew of a new wonder drug that had just become available – M&B. The fever and critical time soon passed and then it was a question of recovering, just staying in bed and resting. What was I to do?

What I actually did was to create my own model aeroplane. My father gave me a board, some paper, a ruler and a pencil. I designed my very own aeroplane, based only on aeroplanes that I had seen. No theoretical knowledge at that time of course. I drew it on the board, full size. My father went to the model shop and bought me some pieces of balsa wood and some glue. I cut the wood into strips and fitted and glued sections by placing the strips, carefully cut, on top of the drawing that I had made and gluing the pieces together. In this way the fuselage was constructed.

Then the wings. I must have seen or learnt something about aerofoil sections, because I constructed wings by making a number of ribs of aerofoil section and glued them to a main wing spar with leading and trailing edges. My father helped me to make a propeller, by laying and gluing strips on top of each other and then twisting the assembly about the axis. When the glue had set, the assembly was carefully shaped and smoothed, making a perfectly formed propeller shape, with the angle of attack of the blade gradually and correctly diminishing as the radius increased and the speed through the air increased. In later life I worked on real propellers and, of course, found exactly the same twist to the blades.

At some point the fuselage and wings had to be covered. This was something of a problem, because of cost. That doesn't sound like a real problem at today's values, but money was hard to come by in our family. My father was not exactly a top earner and, although hard to understand perhaps today, in those days luxuries were few and far between. And a model aeroplane for amusement was very much a luxury.

So, instead of rushing off to the shop and buying special tissue, we used what was to hand. Oranges used to come wrapped in tissue, and, eventually, enough were saved up to cover the fuselage and wings of my model. They were carefully glued on to the balsa frames and then the whole assembly steamed over a kettle to cause the tissue to tighten.

Finally, the motor was made from a number of elastic bands, carefully saved up and joined together. The propeller had a wire spindle that passed through an old bead on the nose of the fuselage and which made a perfect bearing.

Then, at last, the great day came. I was better and my father took me to a nearby open field for the first flight. The motor was laboriously wound up, rotating the propeller round and round until the rubber bands were knotted and fully tightened up. He carefully passed my precious model to me, holding the propeller to stop it turning. I took it equally carefully, raised it above my shoulder, let go of the propeller and launched. It was a miracle. My aeroplane flew straight and level and gradually gained height. It never deviated from its course, just flew on and on and on. We just stood there, too amazed for words. And then, disaster! It flew straight into the top of a tall tree and remained there, tangled in the branches. There was absolutely nothing we could do. As I recall, as far as I know, there it stayed; it was never recovered.

I made other models after that, but none even remotely approached the quality of that first model and the way it flew. I often wonder if it was ever found and recovered by anyone else, but it was probably damaged beyond repair anyway by the impact and entanglement in the tree branches.

Chapter 3

War

There was all this talk of war. War with Germany – again! This was only twenty years after the end of the First World War. It must have seemed so recent to those that had lived through it and more to those like my father who had fought so hard through it in the army and had seen so many good men lose their lives, on both sides; and for what? Here we were again on the edge of another war, with the same enemy, where so many lives of young men and women would be lost. And many, many more whose lives would be changed forever.

As boys, who had no direct experience, we used to gather on the street corner, as boys do and conjecture. Do you think there's going to be a war? But we had no idea of the reality of what was to come. Or that at least one of us was not going to survive. Or that for those of us that did survive, our lives would be changed irrevocably.

By that time I was in one of my short spells at school, Itchen Secondary, making use of my hard won scholarship, all due to the wonderful governesses at Treloar's. It was somewhat miserable, I was not allowed to play games or take part in any sport. Although I do remember once being allowed to be goalkeeper when my form were playing football. But the abiding memory was having to stay with the girls having a second French lesson while the boys were outside playing games. Itchen was a mixed school.

And then it happened. The one thing that we boys that conjectured on the street corner had never thought about. Evacuation. It was clearly thought by government that war was inevitable. It was known that Germany had heavily re-armed and, in particular, had built a strong air force with long range bombers. Southampton was a prime target. I remember seeing the German Zeppelin airships cruising over Southampton long before there was any talk of war. With hindsight it was said that they were taking photographs of the targets to come. I have no means of knowing whether that was true, but Southampton was certainly bombed.

So it was decreed that all schools were to be evacuated, before war started. Itchen school was evacuated to Andover. By then, we had all been issued with gas masks in small brown boxes that we wore round our necks and we were taken to the station to board a train for Andover. So, once again, it was saying goodbye to mother and father – we didn't know for how long or what was going to happen. My brother Peter was with me, but Michael was too young and stayed at home. Every household was issued with an 'Anderson' shelter for protection against the bombs. A sort of corrugated iron 'igloo' that was half buried in the garden. Later, I believe my mother and young brother Michael spent long hours in the shelter.

Anyway, my brother and I arrived at Andover and, with the rest of the school, were taken to a reception centre. It seemed that some arrangements had already been made to house some of the boys, but some, including my brother and I, did not seem to have any pre-arranged home to go to. One of my abiding memories was being lined up, still with our gas masks and the clothes we stood up in, to be selected by potential foster parents and looked after by them for the duration of the forthcoming war. People came and eyed us up and weighed up whether we looked suitable for their home. Eventually we were picked by someone. I don't remember what happened about clothes. We must have had some spare clothing, but I have no recollection of a bag or case. Everything else, of course, was left behind. We were starting a new life with, effectively, foster parents.

The house where our new life started was within walking distance of the RAF airbase on the edge of Andover and it wasn't long before my dreams of aeroplanes took me there at every opportunity to watch the aircraft taking off and landing. I just loved to sit there on the edge of the airfield and dream. And then, one day, at a weekend, 3 September 1939, sitting there, just inside the hedge, it happened. It was just after 11.00am. An armed soldier came up and said, 'You can't sit there, you must get to the outside of the airfield, to the other side of the hedge – now!'

'Why? Why do we have to move, we always sit here, we're not in the way.'

'You have to move,' he said, 'there's a war on now.'

So that was it. After all the speculation, this was it, we were at war. But life went on just the same it seemed. We were at the Andover school, doing much the same things. Nothing much happened. But we didn't see our parents and we became desperately unhappy. We were not very well treated by our foster parents. She was unkind to us and at one point some precious pocket money disappeared from a bedside table. It was later said that it was 'borrowed' and would be returned. Perhaps young imaginations were working overtime, perhaps it was not so bad as it seemed. But I think the novelty of taking in evacuated children was wearing off and looking after two boys was becoming arduous.

But something must have happened. Our parents made a rare visit (for them Andover was a long way from Southampton and travel not easy) and something must have showed. We were taken back to Southampton. The problem was that there was only one private school still operating and my parents could only afford to send one to school. I don't know how they managed that even, perhaps there was some assistance. This must have been early October, just before my fifteenth birthday. I think the legal school leaving age then was fourteen, so I was able to go to work. Thanks to the advice from a friendly neighbour, I was given a job as office boy in Thorneycroft's shipyard in Woolston, within cycling distance of home.

So began a new life at work. For a short while my dreams of aeroplanes came to an end. I was paid 10/- a week (50p in today's money). To get that in perspective, my father was paid something like £3.50/week as a driver salesman for Shell Mex and BP, a job that he hated, but had to do. My job was mainly to take post around the shipyard and some of that was quite interesting. Thorneycroft were then building destroyers for the Navy and during my journeys around the yard I was able to take a look at what was going on. I remember watching some very skilled men forging a keel plate. They would heat it red hot in a furnace and then gradually beat it into a beautiful curved and flared shape to fit exactly over the bottom of the ship. All this, without any apparent drawing or means of measuring. It all seemed to be done by eye, and, no doubt, years of training in apprenticeship backed up by many more years of experience. The kind of training that seems so sadly lacking today, where skilled trades are becoming a thing of the past.

The other memory that left a lasting impression was watching men riveting the plates to the side of the ship. One man on the ground, the other high up on staging by the ship's side. The man on the ground would heat up the rivets in a portable forge until red hot, pick them up in a heavy leather glove and, using some kind of a sling, in one action, throw them up to the riveter at work on the side of the ship. The riveter would catch the rivet in his heavily gloved hand and, in one action, appear to throw it directly in to the pre-drilled hole in the plates. Immediately, someone on the other side would form over the rivet head with his rivet gun. All done so quickly and smoothly. It was a joy to watch such precision and skill.

But by far the most exciting part of my job was taking post out to ships that had been launched and were 'fitting out' to completion. This took quite a long time, during which a skeleton navy crew was put on board. They stayed there until sea trials were complete. And, of course, they had post. A launch ran from the yard to the ship and I was able to go in the launch with the post and deliver it to the ship. It was exciting. Did that start my later love of the sea? I don't know. Maybe. In later life I took up sailing and the sea became my passion. In many ways, sailing seems to have all the excitement of flying, so perhaps it was my substitute.

I must have done a reasonable job, because later – I suppose it was Christmas time – my wage was increased to 12/6. The office where I was based was next to the drawing office and I delivered post there. I discovered that draughtsmen were paid £6.10/week and that seemed an enormous amount of money. So the ambition formed to somehow get into design, although I had no idea how this was to be achieved. All this time, nothing seemed to happen as far as war was concerned. They called it the 'phoney' war. We know now, of course, that both sides were taking the time to arm. There was feverish activity in places like Thorneycroft producing new warships. There was immense activity in the design of new aeroplanes. Aeroplanes that would have the capability in speed and manoeuvrability to intercept and destroy enemy bombers, such as those that would undoubtedly attack Southampton.

There were older aircraft still flying of course. They were often seen flying around. One such was the Supermarine Walrus, an amphibian that could take off and land on water as well as on dry land. It did enter service, I suppose with the Fleet Air Arm, but I am not sure. It was, with some affection, known as the 'Shagbat'.

One day at work at Thorneycroft, someone said to me. 'I think you had better go home, an aircraft has crashed near your house.' How they knew I don't know, but I got leave to go and pedalled home on my bike as hard as I could go. It actually wasn't close to the house, but not far away, at the bottom of the next road. There was this pile of wreckage in the front garden of someone else's house. It looked infinitely sad. Here was this machine, that a short while ago had been flying through the air, like a bird. And now here it was, lifeless, just a pile of wreckage. A foretaste of things to come?

But for me, all this suddenly changed. I was to go back in to hospital for one last piece of surgery that would ease my walking problems.

That last trip to Alton was in 1940 and in the summer I remember so clearly being out on the balcony in our beds and seeing fighter aircraft (Spitfires?) wheeling and turning with white vapour trails left hanging in the sky. The start of the Battle of Britain. Yes, I dreamed about aeroplanes and just wished that I could be a part of what was going on above me. But I knew that wasn't possible. My long held dream had been to join the Royal Air Force, be a pilot and fly. As I said earlier, I used to talk to my father about it and for a long time I couldn't understand why he tried to turn me away from that idea. He kept saying, 'I don't know, I think you should think of the Civil Service or something like that.' It was a long time before I realised what he was really saying. 'You won't be able to join the air force and fly – they won't take you because of your leg.' Or something like that. Trying to be kind, which he was of course.

My father was a great hero to me. In 1940 he had gone back into the army – he was in the officer's reserve following his service in the First World War. I had a visit from him during my stay at Alton and I will never forget him striding down the ward in full officer's uniform. Brass buttons shining and proud medal ribbons on his chest – including the Military Cross, that he was awarded for outstanding bravery and devotion to duty while serving in Mesopotamia (now of course Iraq – ironic that we are fighting there yet again, but a totally different cause). I suppose that I really wanted to follow my father, but by then the reality had sunk in; I would not be able to. I did manage to join the Home Guard, but more of that later. What my father did pass on to me was a strong sense of duty, a desire to be of service, in whatever capacity was available.

After about three months at Alton, I was finally discharged. By then I was walking reasonably well. What an incredible transformation since my first visit to Treloar's. How can I ever express the enormous difference to my life and my deep gratitude to the hospital, the doctors, especially Mr Langston who performed those life transforming operations and the nurses and staff. What a shame that it has now all gone, but I suppose things have to move on – they call it progress, but I'm not so sure.

But while I had been away, things had been happening at home, at Southampton. My father was back in the army and mother was coping on her own with my two younger brothers. Southampton was an obvious target for German bombers.

My parents had some dear friends in Southampton who had moved to Cheltenham and they came to the rescue. I don't know if they were asked perhaps by my father, but the end result was that they were there when it mattered. They suggested to mother that she come to Cheltenham with us boys and they would find us accommodation. I don't know how it was all arranged or what happened to the house at Southampton, but three rooms were found in a house owned and lived in by one lady. There were two bedrooms, a living room and a toilet. The kitchen was shared and there was no bathroom. Washing upstairs was a bowl and jug in mother's bedroom. The occasional bath was a luxury at the Municipal Baths.

And then the bombing started. Our house at Southampton was bombed. Apparently the bomb fell in the fish pond that was just outside the garage. It blew the fish pond and its contents to the air and completely destroyed the garage and contents, including bicycles and a wonderful model of a Thames sailing barge that we had been given by someone – a near neighbour I think. I believe that the whole side of the house was damaged, but, thankfully, my mother and brothers had left.

I knew nothing of this at the time. I came out of hospital and was taken straight to Cheltenham. I have no idea how. I think my father must have had some leave to organise everything. I never saw the house at Southampton again and we seemed to have very few of our original possessions.

Later, Southampton was bombed heavily with much destruction and we were fortunate to be out of it, unlike many others. Some time later I returned to Southampton briefly. I had been trying very hard to make up for my lack of education and I studied hard in spare time in preparation for an attempt at what was known then as Matriculation, the necessary qualification for university entrance, which was my ambition. French was the big problem. I had some evening coaching from a school teacher who was lodging with the family friends that had brought us to Cheltenham. I had to go to Southampton to take the Matriculation exam, I suppose at the university. I must have arrived at the station the morning after a heavy air raid and, walking from the station, passed across the top of the High Street. In front of me a scene that will forever live in my memory. Looking down the High Street there was just piles of smoking rubble where there had once been shops and flats, a theatre and other buildings. There was nothing left. There had been heavy loss of life. I learnt afterwards that many people were trapped and died in the cellars under the shops. They could not be retrieved and the only option was to pour quick lime in to the cellars. I suspect that there were similar horrors in many of the cities that were bombed, many worse than Southampton. Horrors that to this day are not spoken of.

Anyway, the result of my trip was that I failed the exam in French, so that was that.

So, back at Cheltenham, what was I to do? My brothers were at school. I was in my sixteenth year and, I suppose, at that time too old to start school again after having been at work. Whatever the reason, I didn't. Someone suggested that I should look at an apprenticeship at a company making aircraft propellers about 6 miles from Cheltenham. The company was called Rotol, a joint venture between Rolls Royce and Bristol Aeroplane Co., hence the name Rotol. I went for an interview. It seemed to go well, until it came to education. Where was I at school? What exams did I pass? Did I have a School Certificate? What subjects did I take? Came my response – 'Well, you see, it was rather difficult... the fact is, I wasn't at school very much.' And then, 'I see – well, we'll have to think about that.'

The end result of all that is that I was offered an apprenticeship as a design draughtsman, providing I went to college first and gained some knowledge. Specifically, in physics and chemistry. I don't how it was arranged, my father was away in the army and mother had her hands full, but the outcome was that I was taken on at the North Gloucester Technical College in Cheltenham for a six months full time course. I don't know if there were any fees, and, if there were how they were paid, but it was the defining six months in my life. It set me on the road to a full, technical life in aviation that otherwise would have been denied to me.

The course included practical work in the college workshop and I learnt the rudiments of using a lathe. I was also introduced to the art – and it is an art form – of pure and applied mathematics. All in the space of six months, so, of necessity it can only have skimmed the surface, but it started me on a life-long thirst for knowledge. More and more knowledge of the things that had hitherto been denied to me.

And I learnt other things. Important things about relationships with others. I got to know and became quite friendly with a Jewish boy who had come from Germany with his family when the troubles started. His father, I suppose, could see what was going to happen and was fortunate enough to be able to get out in time. I don't suppose that even he would have visualised in his worst fears that eight million fellow Jews would be killed. Even now, after all these years, it is almost too horrific to even contemplate.

But Robert, that was his name, was very good to me and helped me very much. He got me to play tennis with him and gave me a hand with studies. Altogether a good chum. I often wondered what became of him.

After six months I must have had a satisfactory report, because I was then accepted in the apprenticeship and my life in aviation engineering began. It was a five year apprenticeship and the first three years were to be in the workshops. I started off in the experimental machine shop, under the tuition and supervision of a tough, but highly skilled centre lathe turner. I learnt how to use a lathe under real life conditions, making parts for prototype and experimental designs. We started work at 7.30am and worked overtime several nights a week until 7.30pm. There was also extra overtime at weekends. Seems excessive by today's standards, but, of course, we were at war and the war effort was paramount. Later, although essentially the experimental machine shop, I was moved on to production work on a large and heavy turret capstan lathe – a Warner and Swasey 2A from memory. A nightshift was running and when I finished dayshift the nightshift took over. Then, in the morning, the same thing in reverse. We were making blade rings for aircraft propellers, some for the then famous Spitfire and there was competition between me and my nightshift partner as to who could produce the most. The shifts did not quite overlap, there were small time gaps in between and we used to leave notes to each other – sometimes not complimentary. He thought my settings were wrong and he had to take time to change them. Equally, I thought his settings were wrong producing dimensions outside the very tight tolerances required. The truth probably was that the machine settings varied slightly between day and night or, more likely, between my strength and his. We never met.

And then disaster. On this machine the large and heavy turret had to be swung to bring different tools into operation, and to achieve maximum speed this was swung faster and faster. One day I gave a particularly heavy swing in my enthusiasm to go faster and faster and then collapsed with a searing pain in my chest. After I had recovered a little I was sent home to the doctor, who diagnosed a strained heart. That was the end of my workshop training. But it's strange how things work out. When things apparently go wrong, there always seems to be some good to compensate; or perhaps it's the way we think about it. What happened in my case is that my apprenticeship was allowed to continue, but office based. I was to spend a year in the Jig and Tool design office and then go on to the design office, where I would later work on auxiliary power units and marine propellers as well as aircraft propellers. Altogether a most exciting and rewarding time.

Apart from the practical work requirements, I was expected to attend college on day release once a week, plus three evenings. I studied and eventually passed a Higher National Certificate, with special reference to Aerodynamics and Aircraft Design. I later gained endorsements in Industrial Administration. This all took place in North Gloucestershire Technical College (in a different building to where I started out for the initial six months). The head of engineering was a wonderful Mr Skinner, to whom I owe a great deal. His personal interest and encouragement was an inspiration. We always seem to realise these values in later life. It does seem a pity that we do not show our appreciation at the time. How do we know how people's lives might have been changed if we had shown our appreciation at the time? But then, of course, we ourselves do not realise what we owe to other people at the time. Sadly, it's only in later life that these things become apparent and then, so often, it's too late.

On the day before my sixteenth birthday, 15 October 1940, I joined what was then the Local Defence Volunteers, later the Home Guard, the subject of much mirth in the television series '*Dad's Army*'. The Home Guard was always a source of some amusement to many people, but it was actually a serious business and by the end of the war we were a fully trained fighting force. It was, perhaps, fortunate that we were not called into action in the early days. We were under-armed and under-trained. Apart from anything else Hitler had decreed that any Home Guard caught were to be shot on sight. As far as he was concerned we were civilians, and would receive the same treatment as members of the resistance movements in occupied Europe. Execution, no questions.

There was an incident that was amusing, with hindsight although it didn't seem so funny at the time. There was an invasion scare in the autumn of 1940 and we were 'stood to'. One may well ask, what was the worry about Cheltenham? Of all places, a spa town, full of retired people, surely no concern about invasion? Actually, it was realised later that German intelligence was very good and it's certain that they knew full well the significance of Cheltenham and surrounding area. A few miles away there was Gloster Aircraft Co., the home of the first jet fighter aircraft, Air Ministry specification E28/39. That number means that the specification was issued in 1939 and the contract was awarded to Gloster Aircraft Co. to develop an aircraft based on the Whittle jet engine.

That early experimental aircraft was to lead to the famous Meteor fighter, the only aircraft, that, much later, was able to catch the German V1 – the 'Doodlebug' – and destroy it by tipping the missile with the Meteor wing tip and toppling the missile's gyroscope. It then spiralled to the ground and exploded in the countryside away from populated areas.

And then, between Cheltenham and Gloucester, there was Rotol where I was apprenticed, making aircraft propellers, including propellers for the Spitfire, scourge of the Luftwaffe. And, nearer home, in Cheltenham itself, there was a woodworking company that made some parts of the famous Mosquito light bomber. On the outskirts of Cheltenham there was the army records office that may have held all sorts of secrets.

Altogether many good reasons why Cheltenham could have been a target for an airborne invasion. But I don't think for one minute that any of that was in our minds at the time. As far as we were concerned, we had been called out and we had a job to do. I was in a section of ten men and we were detailed to defend a section that was, basically, a large field belonging to the local farmer. We started to build a defensive position in the corner of the field. As I recall, we were given a quantity of sand bags and there must have been a load of sand from somewhere. We busied ourselves filling the bags and building our defensive position, such as it was. We had one rifle between the ten men, and some pick axe handles. There was also a fearsome weapon called a 'pike' – rather like a bayonet fixed to the end of a long pole.

All was proceeding more or less normally and then, suddenly, there appeared this figure in the far corner of the field.

'Look out chaps, here they come!' We gripped our 'weapons' – I think I may have had a pick axe handle – and awaited with baited breath for the whole might of German paratroopers, probably armed to the teeth. We would obviously die.

Then the figure drew nearer and it was clear it was not the German Army. It was the local farmer come to see what was going on. We watched him draw level and as he went by he said,

'What be you all a'doing then?'

'Don't you know?' Was the answer. 'Didn't you hear the bells, there's going to be an invasion.'

There was a roar of laughter. 'Invasion? There ain't going to be no invasion!' And what we thought was the whole might of a German paratroop invasion went off across the next field laughing and muttering to himself about these idiots playing at soldiers.

Apart from that, not very much seemed to happen in Cheltenham, as far as war was concerned. When the German bombing raids started in the Midlands, Cheltenham must have been en route and enemy bombers would fly over. There were several anti-aircraft gun batteries around the town and they would set up a terrific barrage. The noise was deafening and the searchlights and flashes made a fascinating pattern in the sky. Home Guard parades, lectures, etc continued and we were expected to attend, regardless of what was going on above us. I remember clearly walking down the road to go to a parade while the anti-aircraft guns were letting fly and pieces of hot, smoking shrapnel were falling around. Definitely time for the 'tin hat' to be worn! Steel helmets and gas masks were, of course, carried at all times when on, or going to, duty.

Then it happened. Cheltenham had its big air raid, the thing that was not supposed to happen in Cheltenham. It was approaching Christmas. Our grocer's son was in the Home Guard with me and we became mates. They lived over the shop and he asked me round one evening to help him and his father bottle beer for Christmas in the cellar of the shop. They bought beer in bulk and bottled it for sale.

We were working away and then, suddenly, there was an almighty explosion. The bottles flew off the shelf and there was broken glass everywhere. I rushed upstairs to the side door to see what was going on. I pulled open the door and a pile of smoking earth fell in. Where the road had been there was a crater, where a bomb had fallen. That was the start of the great Cheltenham air raid. There had been no warning, but the sirens started shortly afterwards. I suppose everybody was so used to the bombers flying over; but this time they didn't. It was not, of course, on anything like the scale of the air raids on Coventry and other large cities, but around seventy people died and many homes were destroyed in the town.

Local people came in and took shelter in the cellar. My friend and I were in uniform and we sat with them. The Home Guard had no specific role in an air raid and there wasn't much else we could do. But a woman next to me grabbed my shoulder and said, 'What's your job in all this?' Obviously implying that we should not be there. So, we took off and went outside. But there wasn't much we could do, we were not Air Raid Wardens. By that time the raid was in full swing and we cleared up a few incendiary bombs, but most of the bombs were falling in the lower end of the town.

And so the long war years continued. Work, Home Guard, college, not much time for anything else. But my brother and I did go fishing sometimes at Tewkesbury, 7 or 8 miles from Cheltenham. We went everywhere on our bicycles, generally the only way to get around in those days. We fished for pike in the mill pond and down the river. It was not fished very much during the war and, therefore, usually good fishing. A great way to relax.

There were some exciting moments in the Home Guard from time to time. I tended to volunteer for anything that was going and went on special weapons courses. I learnt about most of the grenades that were in use, from the time-honoured 36 grenade, or Mills bomb, right through to some of the weird and wonderful devices that were thought up by people somewhere in the War Department. I remember especially a weird device known as a Fougasse Mine, for use against tanks. It consisted of a small wooden trolley with a compartment that could be loaded with high explosive and a fuse. Attached to the trolley was a small rocket device, rather like a firework. The idea was that you hid in a ditch at the side of the road and waited for a column of enemy tanks to appear. You let all the tanks go through, but when the last in the column was in sight, you were supposed to light the propelling rocket and the fuse, point the trolley at the tank tracks with the trolley wheels on firm ground on the road, and let it go. If you were successful, the trolley would trundle across the road, hit the tank track, explode and disable the tank by ripping of the track. All very good in theory. I'm glad we never had to use it in real action!

There was also a thing called a 71 grenade. This was basically a cylinder of lyditte explosive with a detonator at the end, secured by a safety pin. Attached to the pin was a tape wound round a drum, with a small weight on the end of the free end of tape. The idea was that you held the grenade in the palm of your hand and, as you threw it, you gave it a spin so that the weight on the tape end threw out and the tape unwound from the drum and pulled out the safety pin. There was then a trembler fuse that would set off the detonator as soon as the grenade hit the target.

We were given a number of these for live practice on the edge of a quarry up in the hills around Cheltenham. There were several of us standing on the edge of the quarry and we were all given the chance to throw a live grenade. So far so good. Until one person stood there with the grenade in his hand ready to throw. Somehow or another he managed to unwind the tape and the safety pin fell out. So, there was this man, with a live grenade in his hand, protected only by a sensitive trembler fuse and a number of us and the officer in charge standing close by.

Nobody moved. Nobody knew what to do. But our officer was brilliant. He talked to the unfortunate man holding the grenade and slowly calmed him down. He persuaded him to very slowly lower the grenade to the ground and, ever so gently, lay it in the grass. We then, very slowly crept away to a safe distance and someone was detailed to fire his rifle at the grenade and set it off.

We also practised with the 36, the Mills bomb. Well proven in the First World War. Except that the standard fuse was seven seconds. On this grenade, there was a spring loaded lever that activated the seven second fuse leading to the detonator and the lever was held down by the safety pin. To use the grenade, you grasped it round the body of the grenade, holding down the lever, and pulled out the pin. You then steadied yourself and, when ready, threw the grenade at the enemy. The trouble was, it was found in the First World War that with a seven second fuse a nimble enemy soldier had time to pick up the grenade and throw it back. So, a four second fuse was introduced. The only thing was we didn't have any. So, in practice with live grenades, we were made to pull out the pin, let go of the lever so the fuse started burning, count three and then throw. We just hoped that we did actually have a seven second fuse otherwise the bomb would explode just one second after throwing. We also hoped that we counted seconds correctly. If not...

But in our platoon we had a church organist. 'I know,' he said, 'I know the timing to music, I'll sing this piece and give you the beat, count three of my beats and throw!' It seemed to work.

There could have been a very serious and nasty incident. We had to fuse our own grenades. To do this, you unscrewed the base of the grenade, inserted the fuse complete with detonator, and then screwed the base back down tightly. At some point it was found that there had been sabotage. Someone, somewhere, in the manufacture or in the packing perhaps (grenades came packed in wooden boxes) had pushed a ball bearing with a little grease down to the bottom of the tube in which the fuse was inserted. The result of that was that when the grenade was fused and the bottom screwed back down it would crush the detonator, the bomb would go off and that would be the end of that. We were given a gauge and we spent a long time at base checking all grenades for sabotage. We never found any and we never had an accident.

During a bombing course with an instructor from the regular army, we were told that we had to get to know what it was like to have a bomb go off close to you. We had to get into a shallow trench and crouch down. The instructor placed a 36 grenade on the parapet. 'Keep your heads down,' he shouted, and then let go. Seven seconds later it went off, in my case probably about 2 yards from my ear, with shrapnel flying overhead. Certainly realistic! Later, there was the cup grenade. A cup shaped device was fitted to the end of the rifle and a plate that just fitted the cup was screwed to the base of a 36 grenade. A 'ballistite' cartridge was used in the rifle. (This is a form of blank cartridge, but with a much higher charge). You took the safety pin from the grenade and inserted it into the cup. The cup held the detonator lever in place. The butt of the rifle was rested on the ground and, when ready, you pointed the rifle in the general direction of the target and pulled the trigger. It would throw the grenade probably 70 or 80 yards and was a useful weapon.

One day I was on a course with live bombs and I had to discharge a cup grenade from behind a Cotswold stone wall. I pulled the trigger, there was a gentle 'pop' and the grenade just got over the wall and exploded. Once again, bits of shrapnel flew over my head! Fortunately, the Cotswold stone stayed in one piece. A subsequent enquiry showed that a standard blank cartridge had been issued instead of the powerful ballistite.

And, there was the 'sticky bomb'. Another of these wonderful devices dreamed up by somebody who probably never had to use it. The bomb consisted of a glass sphere about 4 inches in diameter, filled, I believe, with nitro-glycerine. A handle was attached containing a lever, fuse, detonator and safety pin, rather like a 36 grenade. The glass sphere was covered in netting coated with a sticky substance. The idea was that you approached an enemy tank, pulled out the safety pin, attached the sticky bomb to the side of the tank, let go of the handle and ran for cover. You had seven seconds to get clear before it went off. Nobody told us what to do if the enemy tank crew were watching and picking their moment to shoot! The trouble was that the 'sticky' didn't stick very well, so we were trained to smash the bomb against the armour plate.

We trained in a quarry with live bombs. The instructor had us carrying one 'sticky' bomb and walk up to a piece of armoured plate lying on the ground. We then pulled out the pin, smashed the glass bomb onto the plate, smeared around to leave a circle of explosive on the plate about 1 foot in diameter, leave the handle in the middle and let go of the handle.

This started the fuse and you then had seven seconds to run for cover before the thing went off. Amazing how fast you can run when you have to!

One of the strangest weapons was the 'Blacker Bombard' or Spigot Bomb. This was a tripod with spiked feet that you pushed into the ground to make it secure. It had a spigot on which a 20lb bomb could be slid. Behind, there was a firing pin and handles, rather like bicycle handles. Above was a padded head rest. You placed the bomb on the spigot, cocked the trigger and sat on the ground with your forehead on the rest. You pointed the thing in the general direction of the enemy and pulled the trigger. There was an almighty bang and the bomb took off and, if you were lucky, landed about 200 yards away in the approximate direction of the target. If you were unlucky and had not secured the tripod correctly, the recoil would send you backwards a few yards. Not to be recommended.

Finally, we had one weapon that did actually work quite well. This was an anti-tank grenade that fitted into a cup on the end of the rifle and was fired with a special blank cartridge, in the same way as the Mills bomb referred to earlier. This grenade had a range of about 150 yards and the whole device was reasonably accurate. The grenade itself had a diaphragm in the front end that caused a pressure build up behind it when it struck its target. The explosive used took the line of greatest resistance and the whole effect was to punch a hole in armour plate. That was the theory anyway. Fortunately, we never had to use it in anger to find out.

We had other weapons, of course. I learnt all the stoppages on a First World War Lewis machine gun and how to dismantle and clear them, in the dark if necessary. We originally had the American P1060 rifle, but later replaced with the magnificent short Lee-Enfield. I learnt to shoot well and became a member of the Battalion Twenty rifle team. I was actually number six in the battalion, so all those days of practising on the range must have done something.

Meanwhile, work continued. I went on from Jig and Tool design to the design office and got closer to my dream of aeroplanes. I worked on auxiliary gearboxes for aircraft and on a new auxiliary engine for mounting within the aircraft to generate auxiliary electric power. This was the Popjoy, a six cylinder air cooled unit. Popjoy himself worked in the office and produced his designs there. He was in the habit of using a roll of paper on the drawing board and just got on drawing and sketching his ideas, rolling up the paper as required. We juniors had to unravel what he was dreaming up from his drawings and sketches and turn them in to working drawings for the experimental shop to produce the prototype.

It was said that when the prototype engine was eventually built, Popjoy was present when it was started for test. Something went wrong, very wrong. Popjoy was so upset, so it was said by those that were there, that he pulled the old trilby hat that he always wore over his face and stormed off. Unfortunately, he couldn't see where he was going and walked straight into a steel pillar. But, as far as I know, the engine was eventually successful and taken into service. Even in those days, operational aircraft were becoming complicated and much electrical power was required for air conditioning, instruments and, latterly, radar. Sadly, Popjoy himself later died in an aircraft accident coming back from Sweden.

I was later moved back to the main design office and spent some time on detail drawings of propellers, but then was moved to marine propellers. Rotol, were, I suppose, looking for other products with an eye to the end of the war and had taken up the idea of variable pitch marine propellers. I spent the last year of my apprenticeship there and found it most interesting. There were great advantages in a variable pitch ship's propellers, so that the engine could run at an efficient speed at all times. An interesting version was for use on submarines because the mechanism had to be completely silent to avoid sonar detection.

During that time, not a lot was seen of aircraft, except a vivid memory in June 1944 of parachute dropping aircraft coming back from Normandy after D-Day. These were converted DC3's and, for some reason, came back to Staverton airfield, just opposite Rotol, with parachute static lines trailing through the open doors in the side of the aircraft. An emotive sight with us wondering what had happened to the men that dropped from the sky onto the Normandy beaches and beyond.

But, I suppose, the most vivid memory was seeing this very strange aircraft from time to time, that would circle around the Gloster Aircraft Co. airfield at Brockworth, a few miles from Cheltenham and then descend, obviously to land. But it was unlike any other aircraft seen around at that time. It had a quiet whistling sound and did not appear to have a propeller. No propeller? That seemed unbelievable. Surely we were seeing things? But no, it was seen by too many people to be imagination. And soon the rumours went round, it was a new secret aeroplane, not to be talked about. There was a saying during those war years, started from government, 'Careless talk costs lives'. By and large people were responsible and took care. So not much was said.

It was, of course, the Gloster first jet aircraft, using the newly developed Whittle jet engine and designed and built to Air Ministry specification E28/39. This means that the specification was issued in 1939, probably just before the outbreak of war. This then, was the first, followed by the famous Meteor, specification F9/40 and then the Javelin, specification F4/48 on both of which I was later to spend so much time.

Chapter 4

Gloster Aircraft Co.

W e were encouraged to move on once the apprenticeship was complete, I had gained a HNC in Aircraft Design and Aerodynamics with endorsements in Industrial Administration. I saw an advertisement for a draughtsman in the research department. of Gloster Aircraft Co. This seemed a good opportunity to realise my dream of getting involved with aircraft. I knew that things were going on at Glosters, having seen that strange aircraft in the sky. I applied for the job and was accepted.

So, I had realised my dream. I was going to work in an aircraft company. More than that, I was going to work in the research department. All sorts of visions raced through my mind, of research on designs for the future, working at the forefront of aviation development. And, perhaps, finding out about that mysterious whistling aircraft that was seen occasionally flying around Cheltenham and that didn't seem to have a propeller.

The reality seemed different and a little disappointing at first. The research department was in two parts, structural and engineering. I was placed in the structural division and my job was to prepare drawings for linkages used to distribute loads over sections of the aircraft to be tested for strength. Structural testing was carried out in a large structure, known as an 'Abbey' frame. This had been designed and made available by the Royal Aircraft Establishment at Farnborough, known as 'RAE' or, often, referred to simply as 'Farnborough'. Structures were placed in the frame and made secure. Load was then applied, as determined by the aerodynamicists. The load was distributed over the structure from a central hydraulic jack, the distribution then arranged through linkages finally terminating in fastening points on the structure to give the correct distributed load, designed to simulate the aerodynamic loads in flight. Structures could be anything from a complete fuselage/wing assembly, to one component, such as an aileron or elevator.

But, of course, any test can only be an approximation of actual loads experienced in flight and, therefore, a reserve plus safety factor is always built in. During testing, measurements of deflections and distortions of the structure were made as the load was increased. Small deflections usually by dial gauges, of the type commonly found in machine shops. Larger measurements by simple ruler or similar. Later, more sophisticated methods using optical systems have been developed. When all testing had been carried out and results plotted to the satisfaction of the stress engineers, the specimen would often then be tested to destruction to determine the actual reserve factor based on calculated loads. It was just as important to determine that the structure was not over strong as to determine that it was strong enough. Over strength means over weight and, in aircraft, it is of course vital to control weight.

People that work in a research department in aircraft development are, of necessity, well qualified technically and generally give the impression of being serious minded 'boffins'. Not so! There was always an element of fun, creating diversions and practical jokes. One such incident took place during the original construction of the 'Abbey' frame. It was necessary to excavate to a depth of several feet to create foundations and this provided the means for a practical joke. One of the engineers was a serious minded chap who had an interest in archaeology. So, someone decided that here was an opportunity to create a diversion away from the serious and, sometimes rather tedious, business of structural research and testing. With the co-operation of the local butcher a number of old bones were collected and, after everyone else had gone home, these were buried at the bottom of a half finished foundation trench. The workmen returned, continued to dig and, lo and behold, exposed a collection of bones. Great excitement. Taken very seriously by the person for whom the joke was intended and planned. Eventually, of course, the truth came out, but it was fun while it lasted!

Later, another bit of fun almost backfired. This was at the time when there was much talk of flying saucers, with all sorts of reports of seeing these strange flying objects in the sky. There was a photographic studio within the department, used for recording tests, etc. and it didn't take much ingenuity to create a very convincing photograph of a whole squadron of flying saucers in formation! This was done simply by making a mask with saucer shaped cut-outs and dragging across photographic paper with a light above. This gave a picture of flying saucers in formation with realistic trails! More than that, we created a negative in case of suspicions. It nearly backfired, because somehow or another it was leaked to the local press and they became very excited, ringing up and asking for the photograph. We had to back down and deny all knowledge of any such thing. But it was fun while it lasted.

I found the work in that department interesting at first, but I was becoming rather tired of creating constant chains of linkages to apply distributed loads to structures under test. Although each one was different, the principles were the same and it became a little boring. Just at that time I was approached by the engineer in charge of the engineering side of the research department, Geoff Longford, a brilliant and innovative engineer from whom I was later to learn a great deal. He asked me if I would consider joining his team, if it could be arranged. Would I just! It couldn't have come at a better time.

I knew that all sorts of interesting and exciting things were taking place and I welcomed the chance to be a part of it. Little did I know then just how deeply I was to become involved in the whole business of engineering development of the aircraft, leading, in what seems now to be a very short space of time, to being appointed Chief of Engineering Research.

My transfer to engineering was approved and very shortly afterwards I was installed in the engineering office. It seemed that at last I was to realise my dream and become directly involved in aircraft development. I was thrown into the deep end with the first project. This involved the, by then, famous Meteor aircraft. The aircraft had been designed to Air Ministry specification F9/40 for a fighter aircraft using the newly developed jet engines. The problem was that it became necessary to consider increasing the all up weight of the aircraft. There were several reasons why this should be so – increased fuel load for extended range, more powerful engines, increased armament. The everlasting requirement from the services for greater operational features; more speed, more range, more armament to meet the constantly monitored and increasing threat, combined with the everlasting increase in technical innovation in potential enemy weapons and aircraft.

Remember that the Meteor was a military aircraft, designed purely for military purposes to defend against any threat, real or perceived. So, for various reasons, it became necessary to be able to increase the weight that could be carried, after allowing, of course, for the weight of the aircraft structure itself. In the initial design of the aircraft, there is a constant juggle between estimated weight and the wing area and structure strength to support it. There is a limit to desirable wing loading – weight divided by wing area, because this affects manoeuvrability and low speed handling, including the stall speed and landing speed to keep the aircraft in the air. Landing speed is also critical to the length of runway available and the braking capability. So, there is a constant process of successive calculations until the final determination of all up weight, wing area, structure strength, landing speed, etc. Not the least of the considerations is the undercarriage, which has to support the aircraft in all conditions of landing and absorb the energy of the weight of the aircraft descending to the runway. In simple terms, the aircraft will have an energy on impact equal to its weight multiplied by the vertical velocity. All that energy has to be absorbed by the undercarriage.

Accordingly, standards are set for design and testing purposes. The standards specify a maximum downward velocity, but also include a lateral drift that would be caused by the aircraft landing in a cross wind. There also has to be an allowance for the forward landing speed, because, on touch-down, the undercarriage wheels have to spin up to a rotational speed equivalent to the forward landing speed. The rotational inertia of the wheel, therefore, causes an equivalent backward load on the structure. That means here are three forces that have to be taken into account in design and testing. The upwards force due to the aircraft weight and vertical rate of descent, the rearward force due to wheel spin up and the lateral force due to cross wind.

In undercarriage testing the integrity of the design is tested by a drop test on the undercarriage from a height that will give the specification downward velocity on impact.

The backward and sideward loads were simulated by dropping onto a wedge with angles to generate the required loads. This method of testing has several errors. Generating the specified landing velocity by dropping from the equivalent height i.e. by gravitational acceleration ignores the lift on the aircraft wings which is still present on touchdown. The aircraft is landing at a constant downward velocity, whereas the drop test undercarriage is still accelerating. The use of a wedge to generate rearward and side loads means that there is further movement down the wedge to generate the loads, adding to the energy to be absorbed. A possible solution might have been to use wheel spin-up. By spinning the wheel in reverse rotation to a speed equivalent to the aircraft touchdown speed, a backward force would be generated on impact equivalent to the force generated by the aircraft touching down and the wheel spinning up. But this technique would generate its own problems and, in any case, even if successful, would only eliminate one of the errors in testing.

But the main difference that was identified between a test rig result and the actual condition on the aircraft was the aircraft structure itself. The undercarriage is attached to the aircraft structure – in the case of the Meteor, the wings. The wing structure has flexibility and, in itself, is capable of absorbing energy by deflection on impact. This was not simulated, at that time at least, on the undercarriage manufacture's drop test rig. The undercarriage to be tested was attached to a rigid structure that is loaded with weights to the proportion of the aircraft weight that would be carried on the undercarriage wheel on test. So, there were several things that could be looked at in the endeavour to increase the permitted all up weight of the aircraft. The other significant difference is, as described above, that the lift on the aircraft is not replicated.

I think it must have been Geoff Longford, the brilliant head of the engineering section within the research department, who I was working for at the time, who had the concept of drop testing the complete aircraft to test the undercarriage under more realistic conditions. And, hopefully, determine that the aircraft weight could be increased by making use of the energy absorbed by the structure.

There must have been some persuading to do and no doubt there was sceptical management to be convinced, but the project was authorised and my job, initially, was to prepare the drawings for the test rig that was to be erected within the research department hangar. But very shortly, I became deeply involved in the whole project, although the overall concept was that of Geoff Longford and it was his guidance that brought it to a successful conclusion.

As well as taking account of the energy absorbed by the structure, it was necessary to simulate the aircraft lift that would exist in an actual landing. The test rig had two pneumatic rams that were designed such that the combination of cylinder area and air pressure was equal to the aircraft weight being used for any particular test. As with conventional undercarriage testing, the aircraft was dropped from a height to give the required downward velocity on impact. But the rams were arranged such that the aircraft made contact just before impact and, therefore, simulated the lift experienced under actual conditions. The aircraft was lifted to the required drop height by two hydraulic lifting jacks and held by two bomb release slips. This enabled simultaneous release of both sides of the aircraft.

Thus two of the major errors in conventional undercarriage testing were overcome.

But this still left the problem of introducing backward and side loading by wedges, with the errors that this introduces. Extensive instrumentation was fitted to the undercarriage leg to record loads and stresses.

Initial testing was with wedges, but it was known that this was not a satisfactory arrangement and a novel and unique way of overcoming this problem was devised. The wedges were replaced by platforms mounted on rollers giving two degrees of freedom – fore and aft and sideways. Away from the immediate test area energy was stored in a cast iron flywheel spun up to speed with an electric motor drive. A clutch mechanism on one side of the flywheel transmitted rotational energy to a drum, with cables loaded in proportion to vertical load sensed by the landing platforms. The drum cables transmitted the load to a series of linkages connected respectively to the wheel axis for backward load and, by levers in the correct ratios, to the landing platform to pull in the correct sideways direction.

It was a complicated dynamic system, but the result was to transmit the correct loading to the undercarriage on impact without the errors experienced in conventional testing.

The net result was that the errors made in conventional undercarriage testing were eliminated and testing could proceed to discover the true all up weight of the aircraft that could be supported by the undercarriage within the standards laid down. To be fair, it should be pointed out that this was no reflection whatsoever on the integrity and test methods used by undercarriage manufacturers. Tests were carried out on a drop test rig to standards laid down and universally accepted. At Gloster Aircraft we had the unique opportunity, not generally available, to use a complete aircraft that had become redundant for other reasons.

During all testing, stresses were measured in various parts of the undercarriage by strain gauges and associated instrumentation that look somewhat amateurish by present day standards maybe, but all put together within the research department and doing a good job.

So, testing proceeded, gradually increasing the weight on the aircraft by loading with sand and shot bags and dropping from the height to give the standard landing velocity. Eventually, failure occurred to one undercarriage leg, which collapsed on impact with dramatic results. But the weight at that point in the test programme was well in excess of the target and the desired result was achieved. The all up weight could safely be increased, as required by the design office.

After that, everything else seemed very ordinary. Work resumed on routine testing and I was given various pieces of test and development work to perform on my own. Mostly fairly basic, but it did allow me to develop and learn much of the ways of engineering research, sometimes enlivened by dramatic incidents brought about by failure of an item under test. One such could have resulted in tragedy and hardly bears thinking about.

A significant development taking place in aircraft design at that time was the advent of high pressure hydraulic systems to actuate functions such as undercarriage retraction and lowering, flap operation, etc. The higher the pressure that could be used the smaller and lighter the hydraulic components, with the obvious advantages. I was given the job of assessing different types of hydraulic pipe coupling that could be used. The target was to increase system pressure from 2,000psi to 3,000psi. A good example of the detail that had to be looked at to achieve optimum design and consequently, maximum operational efficiency of the aircraft.

To test the pipe coupling, it was connected to a piece of pipe at one end and the other end blanked with a piece of solid steel rod. High pressure was generated by using a cylinder under a hydraulic press, connected to the pipe from the coupling under test. With hindsight, what followed was a piece of foolishness and total neglect of basic precautions. But, of course, hindsight is a wonderful thing! And in those times there was more concern with getting things done than worrying about what may or may not happen.

What happened was that pressure was gradually increased and reached around 10,000lbs/sq inch when the piece of steel blanking rod blew out.

Not far away from the test press was an office with a glass window facing on to the test area. In the office a young lady assistant was sitting at her desk working. The blank was ejected with such force that it went through the office glass and left a neat hole, just like a bullet hole. It passed the seated young lady and then penetrated a 9 inch brick wall, finishing up on the far side of the adjoining hangar. Afterwards, I worked out that it must have passed not far in front of the young lady's head and the full enormity of what could have happened came home. It was an abject lesson in the need to always consider the unlikely, just in case it does happen. Playing the 'What if' game. What if this happens, what if that happens, what then?

To be fair, what actually happened was not the failure that would have been expected. In a pipe coupling of the type being tested, sealing is obtained by an olive being compressed on to the pipe when the coupling is done up. Normally, the pipe itself would slightly indent as the olive is squeezed down, thus preventing end-wise movement. The solid steel blank could not compress and the friction of the olive was not sufficient to hold it under the high test pressure reached.

A lesson was learnt.

Most items under test are taken to failure, to determine the safety factor, but usually failure is a gradual process, as in structural testing for example. But not always so. There was one other dramatic failure with consequences that were, perhaps, comical rather than potentially tragic. Testing was beginning on components for the new aircraft under design. The prototype to specification F4/48, that would become the Javelin all weather fighter. One such test required was on the engine air intake. This was a duct about 3 feet in diameter and about 20 feet long. Under some flight conditions the duct would be at negative air pressure and I was given the job of testing the duct under the design vacuum conditions. The ends were blanked off and a vacuum pump connected. After several trial runs, designers were invited to witness the full test to the design condition, plus safety factor. Vacuum was gradually increased and measurements taken of deflections. Finally the design condition was reached.

Everything seemed fine. I said to the assembled company – 'Seems fine to me' and, as I spoke, I placed an affectionate hand on the duct. At which point it imploded. Violently, and with dramatic effect! Not dangerously, as in an explosion, but dramatically, accompanied by much noise. But the amusing part was that the sudden reduction in pressure in the hangar, as a result of the duct completely collapsing, pulled most of the whitewash off the ceiling and, for several minutes it rained flakes of whitewash!

And so routine testing proceeded. Sometimes punctuated by unexpected events, but always interesting as part of a complicated and extensive design and development process for a new aircraft and maintaining and improving existing aircraft. There was always a constant quest for improvement. More speed, more range, higher altitude, more armament.

But I began to look for more responsibility and a larger scene.

Chapter 5

Dowty Equipment Ltd

During the time of the Meteor drop test programme I had, of necessity, liaised with the undercarriage manufacturer, Dowty Equipment Ltd. on a continuous basis and had come to know some of the people there. It so happened that they were short of someone to take charge of their undercarriage performance testing and I was offered the job. This came at just the right time for me and I had no hesitation in accepting. I worked in the test department and was responsible for the performance testing of all new undercarriage designs produced by Dowty. Not the least of these was for the new four engined passenger aircraft produced by Bristol Aircraft Co., that became famous as the Brabazon. Intended to become a leader in the Civil Aviation world, based on government ideas for a thriving post war civil aviation industry. Unfortunately it was not successful, but prototypes were produced and Dowty designed and produced the undercarriage, which was much larger than anything else at that time. A special large drop testing rig had been produced before I arrived.

I became experienced in the whole business of undercarriage energy absorption and developed techniques for testing. Earlier designs were of the type known as 'oleo-pneumatic'. Basically, air was used in a closed cylinder, inflated to an initial pressure and this supported the weight of the aircraft, acting as a spring. Hydraulic fluid was incorporated in the cylinder arrangement, organised such that as the cylinder piston moved upwards on landing, compressing the air and acting as a spring, fluid was forced through an orifice, thereby absorbing the energy of landing. The job in testing was mainly to determine the correct orifice size to enable the energy of the aircraft landing to be absorbed within the designed deflection of the undercarriage. The kinetic energy to be absorbed is, of course, the landing weight of the aircraft multiplied by the square of the design vertical landing velocity. As mentioned earlier, the figures used are those adopted as a standard throughout the industry.

Later, someone had the idea of using the hydraulic damping fluid itself as a liquid spring. It is commonly thought that fluid is incompressible, but this is not true of all fluids and hydraulic fluid is compressible, albeit at high pressures. So the energy absorbing ram was simplified, consisting of a piston rod penetrating the cylinder charged with oil, thereby compressing the oil and acting as a spring. On the head of the rod is a piston with orifice, enabling oil to transfer from the high pressure side to the low pressure side, thus absorbing energy at the same time as acting as a spring. The size of the orifice was determined on test to just absorb all the energy of impact within the design stroke of the undercarriage. This is the optimum situation that results in the lowest impact load on the structure of the aircraft. Not enough energy absorbed means that the undercarriage would 'bottom', resulting in impact loads. Conversely, absorption in less than the full stroke would, in effect, make the undercarriage stiffer and, again, result in excessive loading on the structure.

Although every undercarriage design was different and each new prototype had its own problems, testing was beginning to become routine. Instrumentation, using an early example of oscilloscope, had been developed and it was possible to make reasonably sophisticated dynamic measurements of deflection and pressures, which made it almost a matter of routine to assess performance and determine modifications to meet the design criteria.

And then, just at the right time for me, a new challenge! Fokker, in Holland, were trying to get going again after the devastation of the Second World War and had brought to fruition an aircraft, the design of which had started during the war, right under the nose of the occupying Germans. The undercarriage had been designed and produced in co-operation with Dowty. It now awaited test at the Fokker factory just outside Amsterdam. I was asked to go to Fokker and help with the test programme. This was an unbelievable opportunity to broaden experience, apart from the excitement of the trip and visiting a foreign country. And more, visiting a country occupied throughout the war.

Remember that this was in 1948, only three years since the end of the war. Things were only just starting to move again after five years of dedication to the war effort. Civilian flying was beginning to move, but, compared to today, was very much in its infancy. The day that I was booked to fly to Amsterdam there was fog. There were not the aids then and when fog came down, flying stopped and my flight was cancelled. So, I spent a night in a London hotel and tried again in the morning. There was still some fog around, but the flight took off. It was the first flight for me and, unfortunately the whole flight was in cloud and I saw nothing. I landed at Amsterdam and was met by an engineer from Fokker and taken to the hotel. Thus began one of the most extraordinary experiences of my life so far.

During the war and German occupation, Fokkers were of course, taken over and forced to carry out work for the Germans. Amongst other things they were sent pieces of aircraft structure for test in their laboratories. The engineers told me with great pride how they managed to wreck as many pieces as possible without getting results. 'Very sorry,' they told the German masters. 'It just broke before we could get results.' They managed to delay the might of the German war machine by a very small amount, but it was all they could do in their circumstances.

And the Dutch people as a whole suffered greatly during the occupation. It so happened that my brother and I got to know a young man from Holland who came to work in England after the war. He had suffered during the war. All boys of his age were rounded up by the occupying army and sent to Germany to work. His family were not going to see that happen and hid him in the attic of their home in the Hague. But there was no food ration for him, because he was not supposed to exist. He survived partly on a diet of tulip bulbs stored in the attic.

Sadly, shortly before my trip, he returned to Holland and joined the army, serving in what was then Dutch Indonesia. He was killed in an army jeep. I went to see the family in the Hague to offer sympathy, but what can you say to people that survived all that hardship, protected their son, only to see him lost in what was supposed to be peace time? That was just one of the many stories that I heard about that went on during the occupation.

Back at Fokker, I quickly organised the drop testing of the undercarriage, with good results, and learned more of the things that took place during the war. The aircraft that was now being built, of which the undercarriage on test was a part, had begun life during the occupation. In between carrying out forced work for the Germans, the Fokker design team had, under cover, worked on a design for the aircraft that they were quite confident they would be able to produce when the war was over. Such was their faith in the ultimate outcome of hostilities. It was a humbling experience to come face to face with the reality of being occupied and the quiet confidence of people who, while in their suffering, were able to believe in the ultimate outcome and that they would be restored to freedom. At that time we were held in very high regard. I was taken to a restaurant one evening and was astonished to have an apology from the waiter. 'I am very sorry,' he said 'we cannot play your National Anthem, because the band are not here today.'

Before leaving Holland, after my work was done, I took time out to go to Arnhem. Something that will forever live in my memory and which has had a profound effect on me ever since. I went to the cemetery of those of the airborne division that landed at Arnhem and were killed in action. I will never forget – row upon row upon row of crosses, all beautifully kept. I wept. So many men. For what?

Back at Dowty, routine testing continued, but nothing ever seemed quite the same. I did receive a thank you memo from George Dowty himself for my work at Fokker, but I began to think of new challenges. Just at that time, I received an invitation to go and have a talk back at Gloster Aircraft Co. The result of that was that I was offered the job of assistant to Geoff Longford, whom I had worked for previously. While I had been away, the research department had been divided into two, there was now a Structural Research Department and an Engineering Research Department. Geoff Longford was now head of Engineering Research, and I was to be his assistant! Of course, I accepted. Here was my dream beginning to come true and I was established in the engineering research business.

Chapter 6

Return to Gloster's

Very shortly afterwards I became aware of the more serious aspects of our work. I was given a desk in the general office just outside the door to Geoff Longford's office. I had not been there very long, feeling my feet in my new situation and wondering how I would be received by the other technicians in the office. Suddenly, the door opened and Geoff Longford put his head round the door – 'Bridge has had it,' he jerked out, clearly emotionally upset. Bridge was one of the test pilots and something had gone wrong on a test flight test. He did not survive. That brought home the reality of some of the work that was undertaken. Part of the Engineering Research department was the responsibility for instrumentation fitted to prototype aircraft under flight test and the interpretation of results relating to mechanical and structural aspects of the flight test programme, working in close collaboration with the aerodynamicists.

The whole complicated process of concept, design, test, re-test, development, modification, re-test and verification continues until everyone involved is satisfied that the original concept and design specification has been achieved. This is a fundamental truth that is as true today in the era of far reaching space flight as it was in the days being described in this book. In fact, since, in aviation, the very first flight of the Wright brothers in 1904. The Wright brothers had the concept, were the designers, the test and development engineers and, eventually, the pilots that flew their creation. Their story is one of the most careful attention to detail and the thorough testing of their aircraft. They even designed and built their own engine, because nothing available would meet their stringent specification. That is why they were so successful where others failed.

Now we have whole teams of aerodynamicists, structural engineers, designers, development engineers and many other specialists, all of whom have to be satisfied that the design objectives have been met. And, above all, that the aircraft is safe to fly right across the designed flight envelope.

But, at the end of the whole process, the machine has to be proved in the air. It has to fly and someone has to fly it and prove that the whole process of design and test has produced a machine that works. Not only works, but does everything that the original specification called for. This is the job of the test pilot.

The department was always close to the flight testing that took place. Over the years we came to know the test pilots, some more closely than others, but with all of them there was at the least an acquaintance and, sometimes a working relationship.

It is therefore, with much sadness, even after all these years, that I record the losses that were suffered over the period totalling fourteen years that I was at Gloster's. Every incident brought home the reality of what we were dealing with. This wasn't just planned experimental work, exploring the boundaries of the aircraft's capabilities, etc. This was real, serious, work with men's lives at stake.

The following lost their lives –

Gloster Test Pilot Lieutenant J. Bridge. Flying a Meteor and stalled on final approach.
Gloster Test Pilot Rodney Dryland. Flying a Meteor that disintegrated during a high speed run over the airfield.
Gloster Test Pilot Peter Lawrence. Javelin WD808, failed to recover from a stall – see Chapter 1
Flight Lieutenant R. J. Ross. RAF pilot attached to Glosters. Javelin XA546. Failed to recover from a spin.
Gloster Test Pilot Brian Smith. Flying Javelin XA644. Mid-air collision with an RAF Hunter.

In addition, we had two near misses.

Gloster Test Pilot Bill Waterton. Javelin WD804. Loss of elevators.
Boscombe Down Test Pilot. Javelin. Loss of aileron power. See Chapter 9.

There was one other incident that could have been a disaster.

Gloster Test Pilot Geof Worrell, took off in a production Javelin from the works at Brockworth to ferry it to Moreton Valence test airfield. Immediately on take-off, he found that the trim control was reversed. Trim control was a switch on top of the control column and was logical – forwards for nose down trim, backwards for nose up trim. On this production aircraft the wiring was reversed. Trim was needed immediately after take-off and, by instant awareness and reaction, the pilot, Geoff Worrell, averted a disaster.

As recorded in detail in Chapter 1, I was deeply involved in the aftermath of the loss of Peter Lawrence.

I have memories of the incident in which Flight Lieutenant Ross was lost. It is believed that he attempted a spin in Javelin XA546 over the Bristol Channel and failed to recover. Nothing was found of the aircraft or the pilot, except for a piece of the pilot's helmet and, I believe, some pieces of the aircraft nose radome. Nothing else was found. The whole thing, aircraft and pilot just disappeared under the water. The Bristol Channel is deep in mud which was presumed to have consumed everything.

But there was always the hope that something might appear and explain the mystery. Since it might have been a controls problem, which was my speciality at the time, I was on continuous standby to rush off if anything turned up. I remember keeping an overnight bag packed and ready to go for several weeks. But nothing was ever found and the mystery remained. Because it was a mystery and, as far as I know it has remained a mystery to this day. If it was a spin, why? Was it deliberate? Or did it happen accidentally? If so, how? And why was it not possible to recover? Was it the same basic problem as the deep stall that cost Peter Lawrence his life? We shall never know. At the time, the aerodynamicists were experimenting with some aspects of elevator control and it is believed that there was a spring bias fitted to modify the pilot's stick force, but it seems unlikely that this would have had any adverse effect on spin recovery.

The worst aspect of this accident was the aftermath and the intrusion of the press. Two or three days after the accident a headline story appeared in the local paper claiming that a bottle had been found on the beach on the Gloucester side of the channel containing a message, purporting to be from Flight Lieutenant Ross, saying, 'I am on Steep Holme island'. How the story got there I have no idea, but, of course, there was absolutely no truth in it. It caused a great deal of distress to the widow, Mrs Ross, who was at Gloster's at the time trying to come to terms with what had happened. I have no idea how the press got hold of the story and how much checking was done on its origins, but it was most unfortunate that it was printed at that time.

ON THE EDGE OF FLIGHT

The accident causing the loss of Brian Smith was different, in that it was a pure accident, but, nevertheless, a tragic occurrence causing the premature death of a popular man. Brian Smith, with navigator Flight Lieutenant Jefferies, was flying Javelin XA644 on a routine test flight when he was involved in a mid-air collision with an RAF Hunter XF980 at a closing speed of 920K at 10,000ft. How it happened is another mystery. There must have been some lack of communication or confusion in flying control, but the result was a mid-air collision. The Hunter collided with the Javelin's under fuselage. Brian Smith and Flight Lieutenant Jefferies were ejected automatically. Jefferies survived with minor injuries, but Brian Smith's parachute lines were severed by the damage and he was killed on impact. The Hunter pilot ejected through the damaged canopy, which caused damage to his parachute. He survived with serious injuries.

The first Javelin prototype, WD804, was fitted with power boosters with manual reversion and in other respects the controls were conventional ailerons, elevators and rudder. Trim was obtained by a moving tailplane with an electrically operated screw jack. It was soon realised that the pitch and roll control was limited. The stick forces required on the elevator and aileron control were excessive. While some re-design and development of the controls was being considered, flight testing was limited within a flight envelope that would permit reasonable stick forces. But even with this limitation there was much that could be explored.

On one such flight, with Chief Test Pilot Bill Waterton flying, classic elevator flutter occurred that quickly became divergent and uncontrollable. In this case, before any action could be taken by the pilot, the flutter became divergent to the point of destruction. The elevators parted company with the aircraft, and the pilot was left with no pitch control.

Flutter was a constant worry in aircraft at that time, by its very nature, not easy to predict. The control surface is, in effect, a spring/mass system, equivalent, in broad terms, to a weight suspended on a spring. The weight, if disturbed, will bounce up and down at a frequency determined by its mass and the stiffness of the spring. The oscillation will gradually die down due to the damping effect of the weight moving through the air and the natural hysteresis of the spring material. But if there is continuous excitation caused by movement of the air around the weight, it will continue to bounce up and down. In extreme cases the oscillation of the weight could get greater and greater, depending on the amount of excitation applied.

In the case of an aircraft, the control surface is the mass and the structure to which the surface hinges are attached is the spring. By its very nature the structure has flexibility. Excitation is caused by the air stream passing over the control surface. The stream will have passed over the surface to which the control is attached, in this case the tail plane, and will have turbulence, which will cause the excitation forces, leading to the surface beginning to flutter. Once this starts, the additional turbulence so caused will increase the excitation forces and very rapidly, under the right conditions, the flutter will become divergent, feeding on itself.

This is what happened in this particular test flight. So there was Bill Waterton with an aircraft cruising happily at a reasonable altitude and speed, but with no means of pitch control, no means of controlling altitude other than by use of the throttle and no means of changing the pitch attitude. In other words, a virtually un-flyable aeroplane. Except that there was trim control. Bill Waterton experimented and determined that by using the tail plane trim control he had some limited control of altitude and pitch.

The critical time was going to be landing, which requires precise control of altitude and pitch angle. He practised by making dummy runs at a safe altitude and determined that he could, in fact, have sufficient control to effect a landing. He was some way from base at that time and it appeared that the nearest satisfactory alternative that would have suitable facilities was A&AEE at Boscombe Down. He radioed base of his intentions and all arrangements were made for an emergency landing.

As far as is known, everything was going reasonably well and was all set for a supreme piece of airmanship to bring the Javelin safely to land. He made a couple of dummy runs over the Boscombe Down runway and then turned to come in to effect a landing. Sadly, something went wrong at the last minute. Exactly what is not clear, but the whole operation was critical and it would not take much to upset the plan. In the event, at the last minute, he appeared to part stall and made a 'pancake' landing, causing structural damage to the underside of the aircraft. But, fortunately, no fire.

We, in the Research Department, had been alerted and were standing by. Geoff Longford, who had flight recorders fitted to the aircraft and myself as the 'controls man'. As soon as the news came through we rushed off to Boscombe Down, wondering on the way, what had happened? What are we going to find? As always in these situations the mind works overtime, imagination runs wild. So often the reality is quite ordinary. But this was different. The aircraft was down, there was damage, but the pilot was, apparently OK. As soon as we got there we went to see Bill Waterton. He was somewhat agitated, not surprising in the circumstances, but the main problem was that he could not open the cockpit hood when he landed and couldn't get out of the aircraft. There was, naturally, great concern about fire. Had the aircraft gone up in flames, as so often happens in that type of crash landing, he would have been trapped in the cockpit with no hope. I noticed then that his hands were blue with bruises where he had been banging at the hood to try and get it open.

So, to the aircraft. The first thing was to check the cockpit hood. We found no problem in manually opening it. We operated it several times, but could not fault it. So here was a mystery. The pilot couldn't open it at first and had, apparently, great difficulty, but eventually got it open and got out. So what happened? It remained a mystery. We then retrieved the flight recorder that was located high up in the tail. There was a conventional automatic observer fitted in the rear of the cockpit that, in those days, consisted basically of a duplicate set of flying instruments with a camera continuously recording. But the more interesting information was probably in the flight recorder, which consisted of a waxed paper chart, unwinding from a drum and re-winding on another. Recording was by sensitive pens with a point dragging over the paper chart and leaving traces. The pens were driven by transducers recording such things as control surface movements, stick movements, stick forces and aircraft altitude, all of great interest in assessing aircraft performance, and, of course, of vital interest in investigating a failure. Although in this particular case, there did not seem to be any great mystery about what happened.

Bill Waterton was awarded the George Medal for his part in getting the aircraft down and enabling the records to be retrieved.

The solution to the problem of flutter was to replace the elevator control completely with an all moving tail plane, which was necessary anyway to provide adequate pitch control. The elevators remained as geared tabs, but with a stiffened structure.

One example of work that involved the department directly with flight testing was that of flight resonance testing that took place on the prototype Javelin. The structure of any aircraft has, of necessity, some flexibility and has its own mass. It is therefore a complex spring/mass system that will have its own natural frequency of vibration in different parts of the structure. In simple language, this means that if the structure receives an impact load from aerodynamic turbulence or any other cause, it will tend to oscillate at its natural frequency, which will vary depending on the aerodynamic loading at the time. The concern is that if frequency were to resonate with the aerodynamic excitation, or turbulence, which has its own natural frequency, a divergent oscillation could result that could eventually lead to a structural failure.

At that time the only satisfactory way of evaluating this possibility was by a test in flight, exploring the whole of the flight envelope. Traditionally, this had been carried out by a relatively simple impact test. A device was fitted to the aircraft wing that, on command from the test pilot in the cockpit, gave an impact load to the structure. Instrumentation recorded the consequent deflections in the structure and their subsequent decay. This was carried out over the range of the flight envelope and examination of the results gave an indication if there was any possibility of a resonance occurring. But this was an approximate procedure at best and a more sophisticated arrangement was devised and put into practice.

A device was developed within the Research Department consisting of a motor driving a rotating, out of balance weight. The out of balance forces generated the required excitation to the aircraft structure. The motor speed could be swept through the whole range of required frequencies. The result of that, however, is that the force generated by the out of balance loads will vary as the speed of the rotating weight. For ideal testing a constant load was needed. Therefore, the weight was arranged to retract inwards as the rotational speed was increased and thereby keep the excitation forces reasonably constant.

In fact, the centrifugal force on the weight is proportional to the square of the rotational speed and the movement of the weight had to be programmed accordingly. The whole device was mounted in the nose of the aircraft and the frequency sweep could be initiated by the test pilot throughout the range of the flight envelope.

Small transducers, in the form of accelerometers, were located in many places in the wings and all coupled to a recorder so that a complete picture of the frequency response of the whole structure could be obtained.

Turbulence and aerodynamic buffeting was always a worry. On the first prototype there was severe buffeting around the tail of the aircraft and test flying was limited to relatively low speeds. The solution was to extend the tail pipe in a 'pen nib' shape to smooth the airflow over the tail.

During this time, the company did not stand still and continued to bid for new contracts. There was a large design office with all the supporting disciplines, aerodynamics, structural, systems, etc. and, of course, a large experimental department and production factory. It all had to be kept going and the company would bid against any new specification being issued.

One such specification was the E1/44, a single engine fighter. The company designed and built a prototype to the specification and some limited ground testing was carried out. It never got as far as flying and the contract was awarded to others. I was not deeply involved, apart from some systems and undercarriage verification tests. I do remember a meeting with Chief Test Pilot Bill Waterton present when he was asked for a first impression opinion. Obviously, he could not say much about the design as it had not even flown, but I do remember him saying. "It will go like a ding bat downhill." Not sure what he actually meant, but it was not meant to be taken seriously. Typical of the lighthearted attitude often adopted, but only disguising the potential seriousness of a large organisation fighting for survival.

Chapter 7

The Engineering Systems

B ut the main effort in the department at that time was the proving and development of all the engineering systems on the aircraft.

Flying controls, ailerons, elevators and rudder.
Hydraulics, for flying controls, flaps, undercarriage, airbrakes.
Electrical.
Fuel.
Cabin air conditioning and pressurisation.

With many complex systems and all interacting and interdependent, the Javelin was a vast step forward in engineering complexity compared to the Meteor and, to complement the detailed and meticulous design, all systems had to be proven for functioning and reliability beyond any doubt.

All the controls on the Javelin were power operated by hydraulic servo-mechanisms that accepted the pilot's control column movements and, through a hydraulic pilot valve and power cylinder, added power to the movement and transmitted it to the control in question. Initially, on the first prototype of the aircraft, similar controls were fitted to all three surfaces; ailerons, elevators and rudder. These controls gave a 'boost' to the pilot's exerted force by a factor of about five to one. In the event of a hydraulic power failure, it was possible, in theory, to still exert force through the dead hydraulic cylinder to the control surface and achieve control of the aircraft, although the forces reflected to the pilot's control would have been heavy.

In fact, it was very quickly found that power was inadequate for the ailerons and the elevators. Aileron control was modified to a full power system, capable of exerting much more force, but with no natural force feedback to the control column. 'Feel' had to be introduced by artificial means. The system was totally dependent on hydraulic power. Therefore, the hydraulic system to the ailerons was duplicated and was apparently foolproof. A later chapter will describe how, in spite of all the duplication, a total failure of aileron control took place and how, by a superhuman effort on the part of the pilot, the aircraft was landed safely.

Conventional elevator control was abandoned and replaced with an 'all moving' tail plane control. The original system drove conventional elevators hinged on the rear of the tail plane. The tail plane itself could be moved about a pivot point by means of an electrical screw jack as a means of trimming the aircraft in level flight and keeping the pilot's control column force at zero in that condition. The aerodynamic forces acting on the aircraft change with speed, and so flight conditions and the aircraft needs to be trimmed for any given flight condition. In the modified system, the electrical screw jack was replaced with a powerful hydraulic screw jack with a servo-system linked to the pilot's control column. The elevators were retained, but geared to the tail plane by a linkage such that as the tail plane moved, the elevator would move in sympathy in such a manner as to offset some of the aerodynamic load on the tail plane movement. It is generally known as a 'geared tab' system and has been in use on aircraft for a long time as a means of boosting manual control systems with no other powered assistance.

In both the new aileron and pitch control systems now installed, there was no feedback of aerodynamic force to the pilot and therefore an artificial 'stick force' system was introduced that would to some extent mirror the natural forces to be expected by the pilot in performing manoeuvres. Such forces are normally a function of the amount of control movement required, the speed of the aircraft and the manoeuvre being performed. They would be the direct connection between the pilot and his aeroplane and give an immediate feel of what the aircraft was doing. Today, many aircraft fly by computer. There is no direct connection between the pilot control and the control surfaces – 'fly-by-wire' as it is known. The aircraft is tightly controlled by the computer and the question of feel does not arise. But we were operating in a different era. In a relatively short space of time, with little experience to draw on, we had moved from an aircraft like the 'Meteor' where all controls were direct to the control surfaces by mechanical linkage, (or even cables), through power boosters, to fully powered controls. It was, perhaps, not surprising that there were problems.

And problems there were. And they had to be resolved. Such complex systems were not, of course, installed on the aircraft and flown without exhaustive ground testing. Test rigs were built, reproducing as accurately as possible the aircraft installation. A whole series of tests were devised, instrumentation fitted to the test rigs and careful measurements made. But, of course, the true aircraft conditions cannot be reproduced on a test rig. Not only the aerodynamic forces acting on the control surfaces but the flexibility of the structure are difficult to reproduce precisely. In theory, the mounting of the hinge points for the various control linkages are rigid and fixed. The reaction points for the hydraulic power cylinders are considered fixed and reproduced on the test rig as rigid mountings.

In practice, however, there is flexibility within the aircraft structure and all 'fixed' points will move, depending on the forces acting. Furthermore, the control surfaces themselves are servo-mechanisms, which means, by definition, that the input movements and forces from the pilot's control are amplified when re-appearing on the output side. So, what we have is an amplifier sitting within an elastic structure with masses attached to the input and output side of the amplifier in the form of control linkages and control surfaces. A classic 'spring-mass' system prone to instability.

Such instability was not apparent on the test rig, but was immediately experienced when the systems were first tried on the aircraft, resulting in a major 'juddering' when the controls were moved, which was clearly not acceptable. Much time and effort was spent on servo-mechanism theory in an effort to find solutions but there are many non-linear functions involved and the problem did not lend itself to a mathematical solution, in spite of receiving much attention. There was concern that it might trigger aerodynamic flutter of the control surface, which is also a 'spring-mass' system caused by the mass of the control and the elasticity of the mounting structure, with excitation from the air stream causing a continuous fluttering, which, in the worst case, can be divergent and lead to structural failure, as happened to the elevators on the first Javelin prototype, described earlier.

It was determined by the aerodynamicists and structural engineers that there would be no cross feeding from the controls juddering to aerodynamic fluttering in this case, but, nevertheless, the problem had to be dealt with and a solution found.

Therefore much testing was carried out on the aircraft itself and various modifications evaluated. This programme continued during flight testing as various other modifications were made to upgrade the controls. It was not unusual to be at the airfield conducting tests on an aircraft on the ground while other flight testing was in progress.

On the day of the Peter Lawrence accident, I was carrying out such tests on an aircraft in the flight hangar and quite close to the Chief Test Pilot's office, which is how I happened to be there at the time, as described in Chapter 1.

Test rigs were constantly updated as problems were resolved and the solutions proved on the test rig. The problem of 'juddering' was never satisfactorily reproduced on the test rig. It was impossible to accurately simulate the effect of the elasticity of the aircraft structure. The eventual solution was to fit a damper to the pilot valve of the 'Servodyne' power control. But, as mentioned above, the controls were eventually changed to full powered control for the ailerons, with no manual reversion or force feedback. The elevator controls were replaced completely with a hydraulically operated all moving tail plane, using a Hobson actuator. Only the rudder remained with the original 'Servodyne' control.

Although much effort was devoted to the flying controls and the corresponding test rigs, similar work was carried out on the fuel and air conditioning systems and, perhaps to a lesser extent, on the electrical system. The fuel system in particular was subject to much development work. A test rig was built of the multi-tank system of one half of the aircraft, the whole thing mounted on a hinged structure supported by hydraulic jacks. By operating the jacks, it was possible to simulate the aircraft in dive, climb and roll attitudes. The system consisted of a number of inter-connected wing tanks, fed to a collector tank located in the fuselage. In the collector tank was a pump that fed the fuel onwards to the engines. There were a number of basic problems that had to be resolved and much work was done on the test rig. But, no matter how faithfully the aircraft system was duplicated, the test rig could not simulate actual flight conditions – 'g' forces on entering a climb or dive, or in a steeply banked turn.

With the system as it was there was no guarantee that the tanks would empty simultaneously. Failure to do so could result in premature fuel starvation, even when there was fuel left in some of the tanks. Effort could be made to balance the system by suitable restrictors in the pipework, related to the capacity of individual tanks, but this, at best, would be an approximate solution, due to unpredictable variations in aircraft attitude and acceleration forces. Therefore it was necessary to develop additions to the system that would ensure that the tanks emptied simultaneously under all conditions. Later, it was also necessary to develop a valve that would ensure that, whatever conditions were experienced, there was no possibility that one tank could empty and allow air into the system.

The first development was the proportioning valve. This was developed by Geoff Longford, before my time. It enabled two flows of fuel to be controlled in a set ratio. Each fuel flow was led through a sensing port, consisting of a disc supported by a leaf spring, the deflection of the spring/disc combination then being proportional to the flow through that port. Upstream of each sensing port was a diaphragm operated control valve. The pressure in the diaphragm chamber was controlled by a fixed orifice and variable orifice. The latter was in the form of a 'chopper' moving across an orifice, such that if the 'chopper' moved across and opened the orifice, the diaphragm chamber pressure would fall and, if closing the orifice, then the chamber pressure would rise and close off the control valve of that flow. The movement of the 'chopper' was controlled by the movement of the sensing disc/spring combination. This could be set in the desired proportion, which was thereafter maintained. The whole device was located in a box no larger than about 8" x 4" x 4", which could be fitted to the fuel system with no problem.

That was fine and looked after the problem of ensuring that the fuel tanks emptied more or less simultaneously. But what if the aircraft rolled or side-slipped when the tanks were nearing an empty condition? This could easily happen when coming in to land after a long flight, for example. Fuel was collected from the wing tanks by a roll pipe in the bottom of the tank, reaching across to each side or corner of the tank, with an entry at each end. With the tank becoming empty, it would mean that one end of the roll pipe could easily become exposed, thus allowing air to enter the system. The system could cope with small amounts of air, but a large quantity could possibly cause an engine flame-out, just at the wrong time. Happening with the aircraft on final approach, turning to make a landing, an engine flame-out at that point could lead to disaster. It was deemed essential to solve this problem.

At this point, I was deeply involved and responsible for systems development. I developed a fuel/no air valve, as it came to be called.

This consisted of a small housing that could be fitted to the end of the roll pipe, containing a diaphragm operated valve. The diaphragm housing was fed from the fuel line through a restrictor, with an outlet controlled by a small float operated pilot valve. If the float was immersed in fuel and therefore lifted, the pilot valve was open, pressure in the diaphragm chamber was below upstream pressure and the main valve stayed open. Fuel could flow virtually unrestricted. If, however, the pilot float sensed air, it would fall and close the pilot valve. This caused the main valve to close and stop air getting into the system. It was, I suppose, not perfect. For example, excessive negative 'g' could cause the float to momentarily stay up, even if sensing air, but for all practical purposes it did the job.

A later chapter will describe how, after the cancellation of aircraft production at Gloster's, the engineering research department evolved into a commercial Technical Developments Division (TDD), exploiting, commercially, some of the work and developments that had taken place within the department, including the fuel/no air valve. Eventually, TDD was also closed and the patent for the fuel/no air valve was offered to, and accepted by, the French company SNECMA. Several years later, I attended the SBAC exhibition at Farnborough and there, on the SNECMA stand, in a central position, was the TDD fuel/no air valve! I spoke to someone on the stand, asking innocent questions, tongue in cheek, but there was no knowledge whatever of the history of the valve and how it came to be developed. Such is history. The moving finger, having writ, moves on...

Back to fuel system development. Tanks were filled from a refuelling point to individual refuelling valves mounted in each tank, that shut off the flow at a predetermined level. The original design called for a proprietary refuelling valve, produced by the Flight Refuelling Co. This valve worked fine for the job it was designed to do, but a problem developed on the test rig that needed attention. The Javelin fuel tanks were located in the wing and, as such, had to be shallow compared to their area and capacity. Necessitated by the constraint of the wing thickness, but at the same time needing to carry the maximum amount of fuel to give the required range. Remember that the Javelin was designed as a high altitude interceptor fighter, intended to be able to intercept enemy aircraft at high altitude and at long range, long before coming anywhere near mainland Britain. The problem with the flight refuelling valve was that the shut-off required a fairly long travel of the level sensing float and was a significant proportion of the depth of the fuel tank. This slowed the overall refuelling time and, also, caused the flow to be gradually restricted and reduced over a considerable proportion of the tank depth. This, in turn, caused some frothing and foaming of the fuel, which was undesirable.

What was needed was full flow over most of the tank depth with a sharp cut-off at the required level. A development of the fuel/no air valve met this requirement perfectly. With a small float, requiring only a very short travel to actuate a pilot valve, all the requirements were met. Prototypes were made and proved and the valve was produced at Gloster's and fitted to the Javelin. (see photograph in plates)

Cockpit pressurisation and air conditioning was by a cold air unit of proprietary manufacture by the company Godfrey Ltd. It consisted of a small turbine unit driving a centrifugal compressor to provide loading for the turbine, the turbine being driven by bleed air from the engine compressor. The air leaving the turbine has therefore done work and expanded and, by the laws of physics, is at a lower temperature. The compressor is taking in clean air and the air leaving it will be at a pressure to be regulated to the correct pressure for cockpit pressurisation. Again, by the laws of physics, it will be at a higher temperature. Therefore it passed through a heat exchanger, the other side of which carried the cold air from the turbine. By suitable regulation, clean air of the correct pressure and temperature could be delivered to the cockpit.

But, it can be seen that there are many variables in such a system and a test rig was built to replicate, as accurately as possible, the aircraft conditions so that pressure and temperature could be correctly set. As always, the only real test was by flight test and observation. Test pilots, of course, carried full oxygen equipment in the event of failure or malfunction of the system. They would, in any case, be quick to report mal-adjustment giving rise to discomfort!

During this period, as the 'systems man', several interesting experiences came my way. The first Javelin prototype, WD804, was entered in to the SBAC show at Farnborough and I was required to be in attendance with the ground crew, in case of problems. (see photograph in plates)

The aircraft was parked in the 'security' zone because, as a prototype of a new type destined for the RAF, it was of the top secret category. In any case, it was to take part in the flying display and, as such, was parked across the other side of the airfield, away from the spectators. This gave me the chance to have a look at the other aircraft to take part in the display. At that time, the display started with a fly past of all the aircraft taking part, the lead aircraft being a Lancaster bomber. The crew of the Lancaster put on their own exhibition during the fly past by stopping three engines and demonstrating that they could continue to fly and re-start the engines.

I thought this was a great opportunity not to be missed. I spoke to the crew and asked if I could go with them. 'For what reason?' Asked the skipper.

'Oh!' I said, thinking quickly, 'I would like to take some photographs.' I happened to have my camera with me.

'OK,' said the skipper, 'climb aboard.' Just like that, no formalities, he was satisfied, just get on with it. If only things were like that today, how much more would we get done? I climbed aboard and they put me in the bomb aimer's position, right in the nose of the aircraft. As I said, the Lancaster was the lead aircraft in the fly past before the display. Therefore I, in the nose of the lead aircraft, was the very first person in the very front of all the aircraft taking part. Even today, I find that astonishing to reflect on. Coming in over the runway in front of all the crowds, nothing in front of me just sky. Amazing!

More than that, on the second run over, the dramatic stunt – three engines stopped with propellers feathered! Here was this Lancaster, flying along the runway, at probably under 1,000ft, on one engine, I managed a photograph. It was actually a slight deception because I could see that we were gradually losing some height, but slowly, not noticeable from the ground. Nevertheless, it did depend on being able to re-start at least one engine.

A production Meteor was also entered at the Farnborough show. I remember in particular one occasion when the Meteor was demonstrated by Test Pilot Jan Zurakowksi. A brilliant test pilot, who performed test manoeuvres with great precision and perfectly timed auto-observer recordings. Jan Zurakowski worked out a 'cartwheel' manoeuvre to demonstrate at Farnborough. This involved diving the aircraft to gain speed and then pulling up into a vertical climb. The climb was continued until the aircraft became practically stationary, still pointing vertically upwards. He then shut down one engine, with the other going at full thrust. The aircraft then slowly rotated, in the vertical position, until pointing nose down, thus performing a perfect 'cartwheel'.

The point is, I happened to know that 'Zura' worked this out in his mind, knew it could be done and rehearsed it in the air only once. I saw him do it at our Moreton Valence airfield.

There were two other rides in aircraft (apart from scheduled air travel) that had their moments and are worth recording. The first was in the Prestwick Pioneer, a twin-engined aircraft produced at Prestwick, Scotland. At that time we were already beginning to look around for possible outlets for some of the developments that had taken place within the Research Department. One of these was in the realm of cockpit and cabin air conditioning systems, as a result of some of the work described earlier. The Prestwick Pioneer was developed as a small feeder line type of civilian aircraft and was flying in the prototype stage. It seemed a good application for cabin conditioning equipment of the type that had been under development in the department. An initial approach was well received and, accordingly, myself and the engineer who had been working on the systems went to Prestwick to have a look at the aircraft. We were offered a flight in the Pioneer to see for ourselves and assess the possibilities.

Of course, we accepted. We met the test pilot and took seats in the cabin. This was, a routine test flight to a pre-arranged schedule. We just went along for the ride and experience and to assess the possibilities for our equipment in the aircraft. What we didn't know was that the routine test flight involved carrying out a series of stalled turns over the sea. An interesting experience, somewhat dampened later on when the same prototype was carrying out similar manoeuvres during a sales demonstration somewhere in North Africa. During one of the manoeuvres a wing parted company with the aircraft at a fairly low altitude. All on board lost their lives.

Another experience was back at Gloster's. Sperry Gyroscope Co., were developing automatic pilots and they had a prototype 'Type E' fitted to a demonstration aircraft. There was interest in an auto-pilot for the Javelin and I attended several meetings at Sperry to assess what would be involved in fitting to the Javelin. Eventually it was arranged for Sperry to bring the demonstration aircraft to our Moreton Valence airfield. A demonstration flight was organised and I was among three or four invited to go along. We took off, climbed to a cruising altitude and saw the auto-pilot engaged, successfully holding the aircraft on course. Nothing more to be expected on what was essentially a sales demonstration. The interesting part came later.

At that time, instrument landing systems (ILS) were beginning to be developed. This is a system that, basically, enables the aircraft to fly on auto-pilot down a beam transmitted from the airfield and make a landing, even in virtually zero visibility. What we didn't know was that Sperry had successfully coupled the Type E auto-pilot to an ILS beam. An ILS system had been installed at Cranfield College of Aeronautics. The crew of the demonstration aircraft asked if we would like to experience an automatic landing. Of course, the answer was yes please!

So we flew on to Cranfield. We approached the airfield and the crew radioed ahead and arranged for the ILS beam to be switched on. Once within range and with the aircraft pointing in the right direction and at an altitude, the pilot switched the auto-pilot to ILS and let go of the controls. I stood right behind the pilot and watched as the aircraft flew itself virtually down to touch down, at which point the pilot took over and completed the landing. The whole thing was most impressive and showed the way to blind landings, remembering that this was over fifty years ago. Attempting a landing in fog has always been the nightmare scenario of aircraft operations – sometimes unavoidable if not forecast and if fuel is running short with no acceptable diversion available. During the war, this was sometimes experienced by bombers returning from a raid, leading to the development of 'FIDO' a fog dispersal system whereby the runway was lined with oil burning beacons of such heat intensity that fog was dispersed locally. But hardly practical or economic for a busy civilian airport. ILS was the practical solution of its day.

As the Javelin developed and the flight test programme proceeded to explore the flight envelope further, various other problems became apparent. One of these was that the aircraft was almost unstable in pitch. That is to say, a disturbance in pitch, in level flight, could easily result in pitch oscillations with very little natural damping. This required constant pilot attention to hold the aircraft steady.

That is a condition that makes the aircraft very unsatisfactory as a gun platform, or a platform from which to launch missiles. The Javelin was equipped with four 30mm cannon in the nose and could carry four 'Blue Jay' heat seeking missiles. In either case a steady platform is needed to ensure accuracy when using the cannon or launching missiles. Something had to be done to stabilise the aircraft. The problem came to the Engineering Research Department to solve and we developed a pitch stabiliser. This consisted basically of an electro-hydraulic servo system driven by an amplifier with input from a gyroscope. The gyroscope sensed aircraft movement in pitch and fed corresponding signals to the stabiliser amplifier, which in turn controlled the pilot valve of the hydraulic actuator. The actuator could be coupled to the pitch control system of the aircraft or disengaged if not needed. The pitch oscillations of the aircraft were, of course, basically sinusoidal and phase advance could be introduced into the amplifier to provide stability.

The complete and entire system was designed and developed within the Engineering Research Department. By that time the department was substantial and consisted of separate electronic, electrical, hydraulic, fuel and systems departments and extensive manufacturing capabilities, 270 staff in all. And I had been appointed chief of the department.

The development of the pitch stabiliser promoted many technical challenges. One was the problem of friction in the pilot valve. The pilot valve, which in turn controlled the main actuator, had to respond precisely to the electrical input from the amplifier, with equivalent accurate feedback from the actuator so that the position of the actuator, and therefore the positional control of pitch was precise. This was essential to ensure control of the pitch oscillation of the aircraft, but it could not be achieved correctly with friction in the pilot valve. Friction can cause a 'stick-slip' motion which would be entirely unsatisfactory. The electronic laboratory came up with the answer by developing a 'mark space' amplifier and control signal to the pilot valve. This means, in effect, that the output from the amplifier was in the form of a square wave. In effect a series of pulses. This kept the valve 'live', constantly dithering by a very small amount, but thereby eliminating static friction. The signal to the valve was by modifying the duration of the pulse in the desired direction, hence the term 'mark space'. It was very successful.

Eventually, our pitch stabiliser had reached its zenith in laboratory development. Everything that could be tested was tested, under all the defined conditions that could be experienced in flight. But now there had to be the real test. It had to be tested, fitted to the aircraft, under actual flight conditions. To my everlasting shame, this led to a situation at its best embarrassing, but at its worst could have led to disaster. The prototype pitch stabiliser was fitted to the aircraft by our technicians and a test flight was arranged with Chief Test Pilot Wing Commander 'Dickie' Martin. When he came back from the test flight, he came straight up to me, looking cross to say the least, and ordered me into his office. I received a severe 'telling off' – a true RAF style carpeting that I will never forget.

What had happened was that when he switched on the stabiliser the aircraft immediately went into a severe divergent pitch oscillation. Quick thinking by Dickie Martin led him immediately to switch off the stabiliser and avert disaster. He was naturally furious that this should happen with equipment that was supposed to have been fully tested under all conditions.

Immediate investigations quickly showed what had happened. In installing the equipment on the aircraft, the pitch sensing gyroscope connections had been reversed. This meant that as soon as an aircraft pitch oscillation started, it was immediately amplified further instead of being corrected. A fundamental error and lessons to be learnt. Never, never ever take anything for granted. Everything should, must, be checked and double checked. Especially where aircraft are concerned, where mistakes can lead to immediate disaster.

For me, personally, this led to almost an obsession to check and double check everything that I do, that has stayed with me for the rest of my life. It has led to constantly playing the 'what if' game. What if this happens, what if that happens. What would happen and what would I do?

In later life I took up sailing and spent many happy times cruising across the channel to the Channel Islands and France. But at all times I was still influenced by the constant obsession to check everything and play the 'what if' game.

Dickie Martin was not averse to playing games himself! At some point during his tenure as Chief Test Pilot, we received some bad publicity in one of the daily newspapers, including the statement that, of course, the Javelin was, in effect, already out of date, because it was not supersonic and had no hope of being so. Or words to that effect. This incensed all of us, including our Chief Test Pilot. So, he took off in a Javelin for a supposed test flight, flew to London, identified the office of the paper concerned and entered in to a vertical dive. Now, in such a dive, the Javelin could, in fact, just about go supersonic. The result was a very loud "bang" in the offices of the paper concerned. Of course, there was an investigation, but Dickie Martin explained. "I'm very sorry," he said (tongue very much in cheek). "My parachute harness got tangled up in the controls." I don't think for one minute that anyone believed him, but the point was made.

Going back to Javelin development, one of the features of any military aircraft is, of course, armament. And that, of all things, has to be of the best available and it has to work at all times and be right. Under operational conditions the life of the pilot and crew depend on it. And there is no point whatsoever in a military aircraft if it is not fully operational, even in peace time. The whole reason for an aircraft such as the Javelin is because it has been determined by intelligence that there is a potential threat to the nation that may have to be met.

Aircraft specifications issued by the Air Ministry (or now, the Ministry of Defence) are designed to meet the perceived potential threat. Recent events in history may cause the validity of some intelligence to be questioned, but that is another matter. It was certainly not for us that were involved to question at the time, particularly at the time of the so-called 'Cold War'.

As mentioned earlier the Javelin was originally fitted with four 30mm cannon in the nose and four 'Blue Jay ' air-to-air missiles, designed to intercept and destroy enemy aircraft. There was an interesting episode concerning the 30mm cannon that may not be generally known. The contemporary Hawker Hunter aircraft was also fitted with four 30mm cannon in the nose. It was found on trials that firing the cannon created a shock wave across the engine air intake that, under some conditions, caused an engine 'flame-out'. The Hunter air intakes to the single engine were much closer to the cannon muzzles than on the Javelin. The Javelin, having twin engines, had circular air intakes further away from the cannon muzzles and the problem did not arise. A Javelin was made available, with suitable instrumentation, so that the problem could be explored further and a solution devised for the Hunter.

The 'Blue Jay' missiles also had their own problems. The missile was designed to be heat seeking. That is, it had a heat sensing device coupled to the guidance system and would therefore, guide itself to the source of heat being sensed. The idea was to manoeuvre behind an enemy aircraft and release the missile such that it would sense the jet stream of the target aircraft, thereafter guide itself up the hot gas jet effluent, and explode when making contact with the rear tail pipe. The problem was, it was alleged, that if the missile carrying aircraft was forced to take defensive action after releasing the missile, it could intrude on the heat sensing area of the missile and hence cause the missile to fly up the intercepting aircraft's own exhaust, with disastrous results. I cannot vouch that this ever happened in real life, but the potential was sufficiently alarming to encourage the Ministry of Defence and the missile industry to develop alternatives, using later technology. In any case, the missile industry, as with the aircraft industry itself, was constantly seeking new technology and advances in design to improve the product.

So was born a new 'air-to-air' missile with the latest technology available. This was a missile with its own radar that could seek out and destroy an enemy aircraft at a range of up to 20 miles from the intercepting aircraft. It was code named 'Red Dean' and was a highly sophisticated piece of equipment. The missile radar could be linked to the aircraft radar which, of course, had a much greater range. Once the aircraft radar was locked on to a target, it could in turn, be locked to the 'Red Dean' radar. All the intercepting pilot had to do, in theory at least, was to lock on to the enemy at long range, fly by radar guidance to within 20 miles of the target and then release 'Red Dean', which then, by its own radar guidance, would intercept and destroy the target.

There were, of course, problems. There always are. Operationally, the enemy target could release 'window' and confuse the missile radar. Or, indeed release any other radar jamming devices. All part of the constant race with technology to be one step further advanced than a potential enemy. From the standpoint of the engineers that had to make the whole system work, the problem was deep, but challenging. The Ministry of Defence (MOD) formed a Red Dean Working Panel with representatives from every company or organisation involved in the project. On a project of this complexity there are, of course, many specialist manufacturers involved, each providing expertise and specialised knowledge and the whole thing has to be co-ordinated. Gone forever were the days when one person could devise and control the whole enterprise. I was a member of the panel, there to represent and to make an input from the aircraft engineering side that had to carry the weapon. There were electrical, hydraulic and air systems required to be fed from the aircraft to the weapon and all had to be controlled to very tight standards. The ultimate success of 'Red Dean' as a weapon depended, amongst many other things of course, on the engineering systems that kept it in a 'ready to launch' state on the aircraft. It is difficult to describe the complexity of the whole project. It was said by another, very experienced member of the panel, that it was so complex that no one person could possibly comprehend the whole system. It depended entirely on a team of experts in their own field working together and ensuring that the interface between each part of the specialised systems functioned correctly. It certainly caused some considerable effort on the aircraft engineering side.

For me personally, there was a downside to being so deeply involved and committed to the project. Amongst many other activities I became a member of the Aircraft Electrical Advisory Panel, under the auspices of the Ministry of Supply. The panel was invited to send a delegation to the USA to a symposium on aircraft electrical problems to be held in San Diego in October 1956. I was invited to prepare a paper for presentation at the symposium. I did so and my paper was '*Aircraft Electrical Servo systems and their dependency on emergency supplies.*' Everything was arranged, but, at the last minute, it was decided by the directors at Gloster's that, because of the critical nature of the Javelin development at that stage it would be wrong to allow me to be absent, even for a short period. Therefore, my trip was cancelled. I was, of course, deeply disappointed, but I was told later that my paper was read by another UK delegate and was well received, so that was some consolation.

But, although the new Javelin aircraft prototypes were coming through, much development was still taking place on the Meteor and there were, of

Javelin, Meteor and Gladiator in formation at the same speed, showing different angles of attack. Ref. Page 5. Gloster Aircraft Co./Invensys plc

First Prototype Spitfire K5054 seen flying at Eastleigh. Ref. Page 26. R.Ae.S

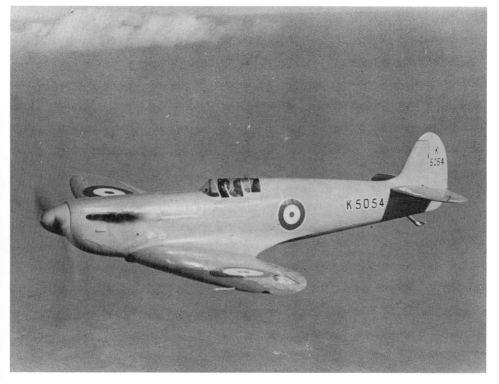

Dornier DoX that called at Southampton for fuel. Ref. Page 26. R.Ae.S

Junkers 46. mail 'plane that was catapulted from ship 'Bremen' with mail for Southampton and was re-fuelled. Ref. Page 26. R.Ae.S

Short-Mayo' composite. 'Piggy-back' aircraft in an effort to save take-off fuel. Ref Page 26. R.Ae.S

Avro Tutor training aircraft seen at Hamble. Ref. Page 31. R.Ae.S

Cierva Autogyro seen at AST Hamble. Ref. Page 32. R.Ae.S

Graf Zeppelin airship that flew over Southampton alleged to be taking reconnaissance photographs. Ref. Page 36. R.Ae.S

Supermarine Walrus - the Shagbat - Another aircraft that my father helped to re-fuel on Southampton Water. Ref. Page 39. R.Ae.S

Home Guard Battalion Rifle Team, author third from left back row. Ref Page 50. Gloucester Chronicle

Structural test on Javelin Aileron showing load distribution. Ref Page 53. Gloster Aircraft Co./Invensys pl

General view of Meteor Drop Test Rig. Ref Page 57. Gloster Aircraft Co./Invensys plc

Original wedge landing to simulate wheel spin-up and side-slip loading. Ref Page 58. Gloster Aircraft Co./Invensys plc

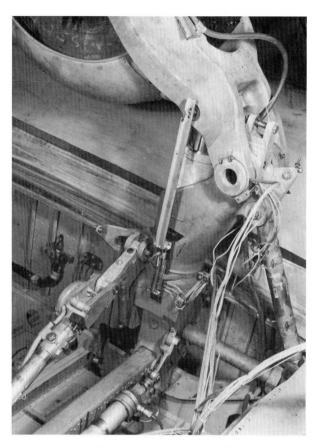

Instrumentation fitted to undercarriage. Ref Page 58.
Gloster Aircraft Co./Invensys plc

Servo system applying drag and side loads from energy in flywheel. Ref page 58. Gloster Aircraft Co./Invensys plc

General view of instrumentation used in Meteor Drop Test. Ref Page 58. Gloster Aircraft Co./Invensys plc

After failure of starboard undercarriage on Meteor Drop Test. Ref Page 58. Gloster Aircraft Co./ Invensys plc

Brabazon aircraft undercarriage drop test rig. Note wedge platform to simulate wheel spin-up loads. Ref Page 62
Messier/Dowty Ltd

Fuel-no air valve, developed in Research Dept. Ref Page 78. Gloster Aircraft Co./Invensys plc

FUEL NO-AIR VALVE
TDD. 106

A Servo Valve to allow liquid flow from a tank but to prevent the flow of air or gas into the pipeline. A float operates a pilot valve which allows a diaphragm operated valve to open when immersed in liquid, but closes it in air. Two valves fitted at opposite ends of a tank would allow continuous fuel flow during varying aircraft attitudes, final shut-off occurring with very little liquid remaining.

DATA There is a range of these valves and we quote particulars of the smallest and largest to date.
Estimated Weight: 10 ounces.
Maximum Flow 1,200 g.p.h.
Pressure Loss: 2 p.s.i.
Estimated Weight: 1½ lb.
Maximum Flow 3,000 g.p.h.
Maximum Flow
Pressure Loss: 3 p.s.i.

Refuelling valve developed in Research Dept. Ref. Page 78. Gloster Aircraft Co./Invensys plc

REFUELLING VALVE FOR USE WITH AVIATION FUEL & HIGH TEST PEROXIDE
TDD. 107

A float controlled, diaphragm operated valve. Flow pressure surges are limited to a small value by the shape of the plug, and valve operation is satisfactory for refuelling pressures up to 50 p.s.i. nominal.
The valve is mounted inside the fuel tank, thus reducing the clearance required for piping between the tanks and aircraft skins.
The shape of outlet nozzle and plunger minimise frothing of fuel in the tanks.

DATA

	Weight:	2 lb.
Aviation Fuel	Typical Flow: Flow Pressure	60 g.p.m.
	Loss:	10 p.s.i.
	Input Pressure:	upto50p.s.i.
H.T.P.	Typical Flow: Flow Pressure	40 g.p.m.
	Loss:	17.9 p.s.i.
	Input Pressure:	up to 50 p.s.i.

HIGH TEST PEROXIDE COUPLINGS
1001/2 & 1003/2

DESCRIPTION
The complete coupling consists of two parts as pictured above, the hose unit normally attached to a length of hose on the replenishing vehicle and the self sealing tank unit permanently mounted on the missile. A quickly detachable protective cap is provided for each half of the coupling with suitable venting to ensure no dangerous pressure build up.
The Hose Unit engages with the tank unit by means of a three prong bayonet fitting, a simple push and turn action locks and seals both units together, and also opens both valves in one foolproof sequence.

FEATURES
A permitted constant flow at high pressure with minimum surge and turbulance.
Pressure loss between units is extremely low.
Spill when disengagement takes place is extremely small.
No special tools required for dismantling or assembling. A fouling pin is incorporated thus ensuring exclusive use for H.T.P.

Light Weight H.T.P. compatible materials.
150 In/in² internal pressure without leakage.
Bore sizes 1″ diameter, 1½″ diameter and 2½″ diameter.

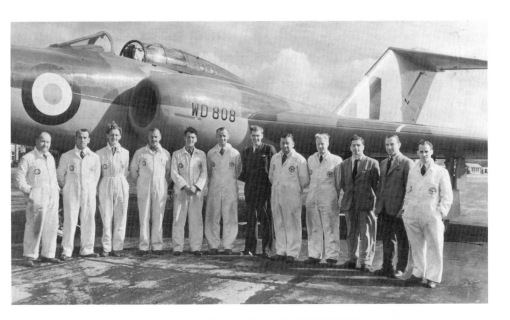

Flight crew with author (centre) at SBAC show, Farnborough. Ref. Page 79. Gloster Aircraft Co./ Invensys plc

Snecma Coleopter seen flying (tethered) in France. Ref. Page 103. SAFRAN (France)

Technical Developments Division stand at 1956 SBAC Show with author. Ref. page 109. Gloster Aircraft Co./Invensys plc

First electronic Self-Service site. Ref. Page 127. Avery Weigh Tranix (USA)

Prototype Refuelling Coupling, designed by author. Ref. Page 139. Absolon commission

Two of the Water Methanol Dispensers in the first Aljac order. Ref. Page 142. Absolon photograph

Fuelling Dispensers built at the Petersfield factory. Ref. Page 143. Absolon photograph

A load of fabricated strainers leaving the Petersfield factory - part of the Iran order. Ref. Page 148.
Absolon photograph

The factory at Petersfield at the time of writing. Ref. Page 148. Absolon photograph

Fuelling tanker for British Airways built at Emsworth. Ref. Page 151. Absolon commission

Refuelling dispensers built at the sub-contractors in Portsmouth. Ref Page 153. Absolon commission

course, many still in service with the RAF. The drop testing of a complete aircraft was a development initiated by the company to upgrade the aircraft, but there were other developments as a result of experience in service. And there were problems with the Meteors in service with the RAF, problems that could not have been foreseen but which led to some serious accidents.

Chapter 8

Loss of Meteors in Service

We stood looking at this pile of wreckage. Fred Turton, service manager, had asked that someone go with him to have a look, with a view to trying to understand and explain some hitherto unexplained loss of Meteor aircraft in service with the Royal Air Force. So I was instructed to go. This is going back a few years before the events described in the previous chapter.

The loss of an aircraft in service could be due to several incidents, apart that is from enemy action. These incidents would be dealt with by normal RAF procedure and, since the aircraft had been approved and received into service from the manufacturer, the latter would not normally be involved. But several aircraft had been lost in similar situations. It was time to consider if there was some fundamental problem that had not come to light in service trials. The first line of contact would be through the service department of the manufacturer. That is why the Service Manager and the 'systems and controls' man from Engineering Research stood silently contemplating this wreckage. There is nothing more sad and evocative to an aviation engineer than a crashed and broken aircraft. This thing of beauty – yes, to an engineer, a thing of beauty, lying in pieces, dead, never to fly again. Never to be able to rocket to 40,000ft or more, to fly at hitherto unheard of speeds. The world speed record was taken by a Meteor at over 600mph.

During the war, the Meteor was the only aircraft in service that could catch the German V1 'flying bomb'. The technique was to approach the V1, get the Meteor wing tip under the wing of the bomb, and then flip it over to the point where the gyroscope in the weapon was toppled and it lost guidance, spinning into the ground. I can remember being at Hastings during this time when my father was stationed there and seeing V1 wrecks in the fields.

So, the Meteor was well proven, a great deal of flying experience in service, under all sorts of conditions. Why now were these accidents happening? The basic reason turned out to be quite simple. The undercarriage was coming down at altitude after a manoeuvre, with disastrous results. But why?

A military aircraft was designed in response to an Operational Requirement (OR) issued by the Air Ministry, in turn responding to a perceived threat and designed to meet that threat. The Meteor OR was F9/40, meaning that it was issued in 1940. That shows how rapidly things moved at that time, compared to today's developments – the Eurofighter for example. Within four years, the Meteor was designed, prototypes built, fully flight tested, service trials completed, put into production and used in service on operations.

But testing and trials were not in any way compromised. The company tests were tightly controlled and monitored, with a Resident Technical Officer (RTO) from the Air Ministry. Equally, the service trials were carried out by the Royal Air Force under strict conditions. All testing was rigorous, exploring every possible combination of conditions to be expected in service, and even some that would not normally be expected. Tests included climate tests, with the test aircraft and crew sent to parts of the world where extreme conditions could be experienced.

So, the Meteor was not accepted into service without a pretty rigorous examination and evaluation of all possible conditions by a number of most experienced people.

So what went wrong? How could undercarriages possibly fall out in flight within the tried and tested flight envelope?

Let us look first of all at how the retractable undercarriage worked. It was operated by a hydraulic ram, selected by a switch in the pilot's cockpit, either 'up' or 'down'. When in the down position for landing, a hinged strut held the undercarriage fully down. The strut had a lock over the central hinge. When in the up position, the strut was folded and the undercarriage was locked in the up position. The undercarriage bay doors closed over the bay when the undercarriage was safely locked up. Lights in the cockpit indicated when the undercarriage was safely locked up and separately, when safely locked down for landing. These locks were mechanical, although electrically operated. It was inconceivable that once locked up, the locks could somehow open and allow the undercarriage to fall down in flight.

It was imperative to find out how the impossible happened and why.

So, back at Gloster's, at base, a series of tests were put in hand using a production aircraft. With the aircraft on jacks, with the wheels clear of the ground, it was easy to run tests on the undercarriage mechanism, using a ground hydraulic test rig. The hydraulic system on the Meteor ran at 2,000psi, with pumps driven from the engines. For ground testing an electrically driven rig was used, fitted with the same pumps as used on the aircraft.

Repetitively selecting 'up' and 'down', over and over again, checking the hydraulics, checking the electrical systems, checking the locks, checking any effects of distortions in the structure due to wing loading and so on. But the system could not be failed.

So what were we not reproducing on the tests? There is one fundamental difference between a ground test and actual operational conditions. The aircraft is not moving. In reality, when the aircraft becomes airborne and undercarriage is selected 'up', the aircraft is at take off speed. The immediate thing to look at was the wheels. These would be rotating at around 1,500rpm when the undercarriage was entering the undercarriage bay and doors closing prior to locking up. It was realised that at that speed, the tyre would possibly extend outwards due to the centrifugal forces acting upon it. By how much? And could this cause some interference or damage that interfered with the locking mechanism? Thanks to the genius of Geoff Longford, at that time head of the department, a very simple method was devised to find out what was going on with the tyres. A piece of fibre board, about 2in x 1in in section, was mounted in the undercarriage bay such that the surface was just clear of the tyre when stationary in the 'up' position. After a test flight, it was simply a matter of seeing how much had been worn off by the extended tyre.

This experiment gave some interesting results and information on how much the tyres grew in diameter. But, unfortunately, did nothing to explain why the undercarriage could come down in flight manoeuvres when safely locked up. Certainly the tyres did grow, but not enough to cause any interference or damage.

The breakthrough came when looking again at damaged aircraft. A consistent feature was damage to the hydraulic ram that operated the undercarriage and hauled it to the 'up' position. The end of the ram was found to be bent just before the fork end fitting. It was easy to assume that this damage was caused by other factors, such as impact damage, other pieces of wreckage, or damage caused when the undercarriage came down dramatically in flight under high speed manoeuvre conditions. Such manoeuvres could easily impose forces of 6g or 7g or even higher on the aircraft. (That is to say six or seven times the force of gravity). An undercarriage coming down under those conditions, with those sorts of forces in action, could cause considerable damage. There was also the possibility of dynamic forces to consider when looking for possible reasons for the bent end of the hydraulic rams. The weight of the undercarriage multiplied six or seven times, or even more possibly, would cause it to come down at high speed. When finally coming to rest with the support strut fully extended, there would be a very high dynamic reaction. Such reaction could cause a large 'bounce back' that could easily have caused the damage to the ram.

Fine, a plausible theory, but it still didn't explain why the undercarriage came down in the first place. This was a mystery that had to be resolved. These were not experimental aircraft, or aircraft carrying out special test manoeuvres. These were tried and tested aircraft in service with the Royal Air Force, carrying out legitimate flying exercises within the permitted flight envelope. The flight envelope defines the limit of conditions under which the aircraft is permitted to operate in a safe regime. It will define such things as maximum speed, maximum 'g' loadings, minimum stalling speed and so on. Limits to be applied in normal operations, but obviously disregarded at times under real combat conditions in hostile situations. That was a matter for the Air Force and pilots. It was clearly totally unacceptable that this present situation could continue, with the possibility of loss of life and loss of aircraft.

So, back to square one. Let's look at the problem from a different perspective. Supposing the ram was already bent before any operation started? What would be the effect? Back to tests on an aircraft in the hangar on jacks, with the undercarriage clear of the ground. Fit a ram with the end bent as in the unit found in the wreckage. Select 'up'. Hey presto! The undercarriage failed to lock up. This meant that there was nothing to hold it up except the ram itself. Under high 'g' conditions it would certainly come down.

But how could this possibly be? It seemed inconceivable that an aircraft regularly serviced could have bent hydraulic rams and go unnoticed. In any case, the cockpit lights would have indicated quite clearly that safe lock up had not been achieved after take-off. The fact remained that the rams were bent. This meant that the undercarriage could not have been locked up. This meant that it would certainly come down under some flight conditions.

Time to talk to the men in blue that actually flew the aircraft.

Since the aircraft were in service with the Royal Air Force, this was a matter for the Service Department. The Service Manager, Fred Turton, therefore visited stations where this problem had occurred. Gradually, the truth came out. First of all, the answer to the question. 'We know that there was damage to the undercarriage mechanism that would have made it impossible for the undercarriage to be safely locked up. But the undercarriage indicator lights would have made this clear and the flight would have been abandoned – wouldn't it?'

'Well yes, but ...' But what?

'But the lights were sometimes not working properly,' or, 'the indicator light must have been faulty, because you could hear the undercarriage locking up, so it was ignored.'

Fine, except that, as we now know, the gear was not locked up and subsequently came down in manoeuvres. Too late then to say the lights were right after all, and too embarrassed perhaps to admit it. As far as I know, nothing much was said at the time. The pilots that fly these things in the RAF obviously have many disciplines, many tasks to perform on an operational mission. A strong desire to get airborne and up to operational height as soon as possible. It is easy to understand that a warning light that may well be perceived as being unreliable, could be ignored as being a relatively minor matter compared to the task on hand.

That was one part of the problem explained, but what about the bent hydraulic jack? That was the fundamental mystery. If the jack had not been bent in the first place, the undercarriage would have safely locked up regardless of what the lights showed. It was apparent that the damage must have been caused on the same flight as the undercarriage coming down. It was inconceivable that that sort of damage could have gone unnoticed on successive flights. The gear would not lock down properly, apart from anything else. And it would have been picked up on pre-flight inspections. So, it occurred on the same flight. But how? It could only be caused by a large load acting on the wheels with the undercarriage unlocked. And the undercarriage could only be unlocked by selecting 'up' after take-off, but after take-off there would be no load on the wheels. Therefore, there was only one possible explanation. There was an imposed load on the wheels after selection, and in such a manner as to cause a sideways load sufficient to bend the end of the hydraulic jack. Back to the men in blue.

The final explanation was what became known as a 'brush take off'. The same kind of enthusiastic scenario that enabled warning lights to be ignored caused the bent jacks. In the strong and enthusiastic desire to get airborne and away as soon as possible after scrambling, it became practice to select 'up' before becoming airborne. As soon as weight was off the wheels, the undercarriage would then retract, giving the minimum time to get off the ground with a 'clean' aircraft. That would have been fine and would normally work. Unfortunately, there were occasions when, just after becoming airborne, the aircraft would sink slightly and the wheels would touch again with the undercarriage unlocked. Often with a slight sideslip, thereby imposing a side load which would easily cause the damage seen on the hydraulic jacks, and as shown in the illustration. So, there it was, the answer to the mystery.

As is so often the case, the accidents therefore were a combination of two things happening together. A 'brush take off' followed by ignoring the

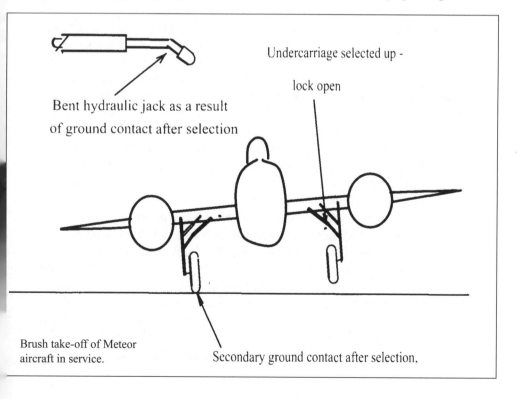

Undercarriage selected up -

lock open

Bent hydraulic jack as a result of ground contact after selection

Brush take-off of Meteor aircraft in service.

Secondary ground contact after selection.

warning lights. There have been several recorded accidents caused, it is believed, by instruments being ignored or believed to be incorrect. It seems to be a basic human reaction in cases of doubt to rely on instinctive feelings born out of experience, rather than trust a mechanical device. It is unfortunate that the mechanical device is so often more reliable. But, as we all know, there are occasions when the mechanical device or instrument is in fact at fault. The problem for anyone in charge of a piece of machinery as complicated as a modern jet fighter at that time, must be how to know the difference.

And then there was the problem with the fuel system. There were a number of unexplained accidents on the Meteor when coming in to land on final approach. It seemed that there was a sudden loss of power on both engines, just at the critical point on 'finals', causing loss of control of the aircraft. It became apparent that the only explanation could be a fuel shortage on both engines. But it was found that there was fuel left in the tanks. So what happened?

Another mystery to be solved by painstaking tests in the Research Department.

A test rig was built, using actual Meteor fuel tanks and controls, the whole mounted on a frame that could be tilted to represent flight conditions.

The basic layout of the fuel system is shown in the diagram. It will be seen that there were two tanks, located in the fuselage and arranged in tandem, one normally feeding the port engine and the other the starboard engine. The tanks were connected by a balance pipe, the reason being to balance out the tank contents when in level flight, thus optimising the use of fuel and consequently the range of the aircraft. There was a cross feed arrangement that, when selected, enabled fuel to be fed to the opposite engine in the event that a tank ran dry. That is, it connected the tank with fuel left to both engines.

Tests were carried out simulating a typical flight pattern with climb and roll attitudes. The test rig was constructed such that fuel could be taken from the tanks at the rate of flow associated with the flight pattern at any particular time. Records were kept of observations made and the amount of fuel left in each tank at the end of the simulated flight pattern. Everything seemed more or less normal and there was enough fuel left to complete the flight pattern. But what is a normal flight pattern? The conventional operational sortie was well defined. Take off, climb to operational altitude, mission, descend, land. But suppose there was another flight pattern, not the

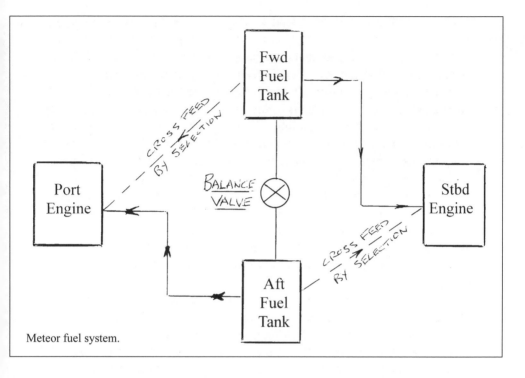

Meteor fuel system.

'standard' operational sortie, but a variation? So a whole sequence of other flight patterns were investigated.

Eventually, a pattern evolved that could give trouble. Take off, prolonged climb to maximum altitude, cruise at low speed and therefore at a high angle of incidence, descend and land. The angle of incidence would be high due to the high altitude and the aircraft operating virtually at its maximum altitude and therefore close to the stall. This meant that the aircraft was in a nose up attitude for most of the flight.

The tests showed all too clearly that the result was that the forward tank discharged into the rear tank through the balance pipe and became empty just before the end of the flight. This meant that the engine being fed from that tank would go out. But what about the cross feed system? The whole point of the system was that in exactly the circumstances being simulated on the test rig, when the engine failed being fed from the forward tank, cross feed would be selected from the remaining tank so that it would feed both engines. In fact, cross feed could be selected when the tank gauge showed a near empty condition, thus avoiding having to re-start the dead engine.

The reality was that cross feed was selected and the remaining engine promptly cut out.

There was only one logical explanation for that to have happened. I do not recall the full details of the cross-feed system, but it was clear that cross-feed and, possibly, some combination of crossfeed and tank balance valve, was selected incorrectly. That is to say, in error, the cross feed of the empty tank was selected, thereby cutting off fuel to the remaining engine. It was unfortunate that this so often happened right at the end of an operation, on final approach, when there was no time left to appreciate what had happened and to rectify the situation.

I do not remember what the final solution was, but it almost certainly involved clearer labelling, possibly re-positioning of the cross feed controls to more readily identify them with the relevant tank/engine and more training. Whatever the solution was, the problem was dealt with by painstaking testing and re-testing until it had been dealt with to everyone's satisfaction.

It is interesting to recall one of the fundamentals of development testing. It might be thought that the test engineer spends his time trying to prove that things work. The fact is, that although that is the long term objective, the immediate objective is to try to make it not work. Or, in the case of a structure, to try and break it. And to devise modifications that, no matter how hard one tries, within the defined envelope, it will work and will not break. That is the only way to ensure that it will do the job that it is designed to do.

Chapter 9

The Boscombe Down Incident

As development of any new military aircraft proceeded it was necessary for the service for which it was intended to be able to assess the aircraft in the prototype stage, before production could be authorised to proceed. A number of prototype aircraft are built initially, six in the case of the Javelin, and one of these was sent to the Aircraft and Armament Experimental Establishment (A&AEE) based at Boscombe Down. Royal Air Force test pilots there carried out a series of trials to determine the suitability of the aircraft for service use. This would be different to the tests carried out by the company test pilots. Such tests were designed to explore the flight envelope under various conditions and determine that the aircraft met the design parameters, followed, if necessary, by development tests to determine the success or otherwise of modifications that had been introduced as a result of initial tests. In general, the company would determine that the aircraft met the specification.

The flight trials by the RAF at Boscombe Down were designed to evaluate the aircraft under service conditions and check performance against operational requirements. On one such flight trial the theoretically impossible happened. There was a total failure of hydraulic power to the aileron controls.

The original prototype had a power boost system on all the flying controls, consisting of a device known as a 'Servodyne'. This was necessary because the predicted forces on the controls would be more than the pilot could exert, by a factor approaching five. In effect, the device multiplied the manual input from the pilot by a factor of five. That is to say if the control needed a force at the cockpit control column of x then the pilot would only feel a force of x/5, the rest being provided by the hydraulics, but always in the correct proportion, so that the forces felt by the pilot would feel natural. If there was a hydraulic failure the system could still be used in a manual mode, but flight speed would have to be reduced to give manageable 'stick' forces. However, early flight testing quickly showed that the control forces were much higher than expected and the system had to be replaced.

Initially, the aileron control was found to be the control giving by far the highest stick forces and this was replaced at an early stage by a fully powered system. This gave no feedback to the pilot of control forces and an artificial feel system was introduced. The difficulty with such a system is that there is no manual reversion. Therefore the hydraulic supply to the aileron control was duplicated. There were two hydraulic pumps fitted to the auxiliary gearbox to serve all the general hydraulic systems on the aircraft and a supply was taken from each pump to power the ailerons. Each supply went to a shuttle valve that was biased to allow supply from one of the pumps through to the aileron actuators, and was held in that position by the pressure in the circuit. In the event of a failure of the primary supply, the shuttle valve would be unbalanced and would automatically admit pressure from the second pump into the circuit.

On the flight in question, something went wrong. There was a total failure of power to the aileron control. This meant that, without aileron control it would be impossible to bank the aircraft, which is necessary in order to turn. Rudder and elevator control were still available, but without ailerons directional control would be virtually impossible. Certainly to attempt a landing would have been courting disaster. But, by some superhuman effort, the pilot managed to gain some control and successfully landed. How he did it still remains something of a mystery. He would have had to be able by some means, to transmit sufficient load through the control linkage to be able to move the piston in the power control cylinder, overcoming friction in the system and displacing hydraulic fluid.

In any event, it was a control problem and it was my job to go to Boscombe Down, determine what had gone wrong and why, followed by putting it right! The first step was to interview the pilot. This was very difficult for me. Here was this man in blue, who had put his life on the line and achieved what by many standards was an impossible task in successfully landing a disabled aircraft rather than bail out. Had he ejected, the aircraft would have been lost and the secret of what went wrong probably buried in the wreckage forever. Who was I to ask this man questions about what he did? But we had to determine the problem and find out what happened. In the event, he couldn't tell us very much. He confirmed that he was only able to have some sort of roll control by a massive effort. He had to jam his leg against the side of the cockpit and use all his strength to achieve some movement of the ailerons.

There was a question about the timing. When did the failure actually occur? And how long did he struggle? This could be significant because, matched against the flight plan, it could determine altitude at the time, which might be a factor. In any case, in an investigation of this sort we need to know all the facts. Any piece of information, no matter how small, might be a clue as to what happened. The pilot, naturally, could not be very helpful on this aspect. He had his hands full in coping with the aircraft. It is difficult to imagine the magnitude of the problem, to those that have not experienced it. And then, it was remembered. The aircraft was fitted with a voice recorder to record everything that was said by the pilot during the flight. So the pilot was asked to go and get the wire tape so we could listen and match events against a time base.

After a while he returned. In his hands was a complete tangle of wire draped across his outstretched arms and hands.

'I'm so sorry,' he said, 'it tangled up when I tried to take it out of the recorder.'

There was, of course, nothing that we could do. There was no way in which any information could be obtained from the wire. Perhaps it was just as well. This was a cockpit voice recorder and would contain anything that the pilot would have said during the tense, traumatic time that he was struggling with the aircraft. It would not be surprising if he was actually quite relieved that whatever words he may or may not have uttered were not to be heard by others.

Just recently I have learned the pilot's name and I am pleased to record that it was Air Commodore John Sowery and he was later awarded the Air Force Cross.

But the problem remained. What happened and why? A solution had to be found, otherwise it could happen again. I was given a free hand to investigate. I was booked in to a local hotel and told that I could have sent to Boscombe anything that I needed to carry out investigative tests and to take my time – whatever time was necessary. Great credit is due to the directors and senior management at Gloster's that had the confidence and gave me the freedom to find a solution.

The fundamental requirement was to be able to operate the hydraulic systems and, hopefully, reproduce the failure. There was a standard test rig at Gloster's that consisted of an electric motor driving the same type of hydraulic pump fitted to the aircraft, so I had that sent down, together with various instruments, gauges, etc., that I would need for the investigation. The aircraft was moved to a hangar where I would not be disturbed and mounted on jacks. I was left alone to get on with it, but with the assurance that if there was anything I needed it would be forthcoming. With the aircraft on jacks, the hydraulic test rig was connected into the aircraft system and I was all set to start testing. All the systems were checked: Aileron, elevator and rudder movement; undercarriage retracted and lowered; every possible combination of movements to check if there was any interaction between the systems that could lead to a malfunction. But, whatever I did, everything worked normally. The failure of the aileron control could not be reproduced. So what next?

Back to looking at the whole system. As explained earlier, the whole hydraulic system was duplicated, with an automatic changeover device in the event of failure of one pump. Everything was duplicated except one item, the oil reservoir that fed the pumps. Whatever else was taking place, there was only one supply of oil. True, the reservoir was partially divided down the centre to separate the supply to each pump, but with a common air space at the top. So, the focus had to be on that one common item.

Unfortunately, some of the detail is lost in the mists of time, but I was looking at the possibility that there was a loss of pressure in one circuit, which caused the shuttle valve to switch to the duplicated circuit. But, at the same time, the half of the reservoir feeding the standby circuit lost oil because it was displaced to the shut down side of the reservoir. A contributory factor could have been aeration and foaming of the oil due to altitude and turbulence.

This was a very difficult thing to prove with a ground test rig, but I became convinced that the correct remedy was to have fully separated reservoirs for each hydraulic system, so that there was no possibility of an interchange of oil taking place. So back to the designers at Gloster's to explain my theory and ask for modifications to the system accordingly. My theory was accepted and a new oil reservoir designed with fully separated, sealed, compartments for each half of the hydraulic system. A new reservoir was quickly made up and installed on the aircraft waiting at Boscombe Down. All the tests that had been carried out were repeated and every effort made to fail the system. But everything worked correctly, although it was not possible to simulate altitude conditions. Nevertheless, I was convinced that the answer had been found and a solution applied.

Then, the aircraft was to go back to the Gloster airfield at Moreton Valence, just outside Gloucester. The Chief Test Pilot, Bill Waterton came down to fly the aircraft back. He went straight to the pilot's office and sent for me. He did not even stop to look at the aircraft, which was flight ready. I went to the office, not quite sure what to expect. I certainly did not expect what followed. Bill Waterton was there and he appeared to be in something of a state. He was sweating and was obviously very agitated. He looked straight at me and jerked out.

'Is this thing safe to fly?'

That was a defining moment in my life. Here was this aeroplane that had experienced a total failure of a powered flying control with no manual reversion that, by some miracle had been landed by an RAF test pilot. A pilot who, if he had so wished, could have ejected and abandoned the aircraft, in which case we would never have known what happened. An aircraft that had been tested, modified and re-tested. But with a diagnosed fault that was almost impossible to prove was the cause of the failure.

And here was our chief test pilot, confronting me – 'Is this thing safe to fly?'

There had to be a reply immediately. No hesitation. 'Yes, Bill, it's OK.' Bill Waterton looked me straight in the eye, with a finger pointing directly at me. 'Then be it on your head.'

The words were jerked out, with those eyes still looking straight at me. Words that will live in my mind forever.

With that, he turned on his heel and walked straight over to where the Javelin stood flight ready. He climbed in and the ground crew removed the boarding ladder. He started the engines and with no delay taxied to the end of the runway. Opened to full throttle and took off.

I watched as he climbed away, banked and turned. He came back down the runway at full speed and zero feet. I watched in sheer disbelief as he proceeded to carry out full rolls the whole way down the runway and then climbed away and headed for Gloucester. Remember it was a failure of the aileron control that had occurred and it is the ailerons that are used in rolling. Had there been any fault in the controls during the manoeuvre I had just witnessed it would have been goodbye. Goodbye Bill, goodbye Javelin. There would have been nothing left.

What follows is second hand. I was not witness to the subsequent events that are reputed to have happened. But I was assured by others that this is what happened. It was said that Bill Waterton flew the Javelin back to Moreton Valence, virtually hedge hopping all the way back. He landed, jumped into his car and drove straight to the office at Brockworth, the other side of Gloucester. He went straight up to the Managing Director's office, threw his flying gloves on the table and said. 'That's it, I quit.'

That was the story, but, as I say, I have no means of verifying it. I only know what happened at Boscombe Down, but certainly there was a great deal of tension over the whole incident. It was said that he gave up test flying altogether, but, again, I have no personal knowledge of that. Certainly he left Gloster's and was replaced by a new Chief Test Pilot, Dickie Martin.

Whatever the truth of the aftermath of the incident at Boscombe Down, there is no question that, in those years, test flying was a very hazardous and tense business. It is not in the least surprising that tensions are released in ways that in normal circumstances would be considered abnormal behaviour.

Chapter 10

The Time of Change

While all this was going on with the Javelin and Meteors in service, the future was not forgotten. R. W. Walker, chief designer, and his team were working on a Javelin replacement to Air Ministry specification F153D. This would be a thin wing version, capable of supersonic speeds. The 'thin wing' concept was, fundamentally, to reduce drag and improve stability and aerodynamic characteristics in the transonic and supersonic range. The design was far advanced and some components of a prototype were being produced in the workshops. We in Research were not involved at that stage, but were aware, of course, of what was taking place for the future.

Talking of the future, at that time there was, of course, great interest in any new development anywhere in the world, particularly in military aviation. At some point I found myself at SNECMA, the French aircraft engine company, probably following up some new development of interest to us at Gloster. SNECMA were very kind and welcoming and took great pride in showing me their latest development. This was a circular wing aircraft, designed for vertical take-off and revolutionary for its time and of great significance at that time for military use in forward combat areas, where take-off and landing could take place in confined spaces, giving great back-up for forward operating ground forces. It was basically a flying engine – a SNECMA engine of course. A unique photograph of the machine flying (although tethered in case of problems!) is shown in the photograph section.

There had been talk for some time of a possible scaling down of defence expenditure nationally. The cold war seemed to be coming to an end and the threat that had driven so much development in military equipment appeared to be receding. But I don't think anyone was prepared for what actually happened. Suddenly, without any warning, a large number of defence contracts were cancelled. Among those in the aircraft industry were the TSR2 and the thin wing Javelin – the F153D. The loss of the TSR2 development in particular had devastating consequences. It was far advanced and was at the cutting edge of supersonic technology. The British aircraft industry was on the point of becoming a world leader in aviation technology and suddenly, it was lost. It took many years to partially recover but nothing seemed to be the same afterwards.

Development at Gloster Aircraft Co. was a part of the surge in technology that was taking place and the supersonic F153D project was the way to the future. But suddenly it all changed. I remember so clearly being at a meeting with others in the chief designer's office shortly after the news came through. R. W. Walker (Dickie) as he was known, was completely devastated. 'It was all happening,' he said, voice breaking. 'The wing spars were being milled down in the factory, everything getting ready for the prototype and now it's all for nothing.' I don't think he ever really recovered from that. I felt for him deeply. He had always been so supportive to me and had encouraged my every step. And, of course, everyone was going to be affected. What was to happen now?

There was work to complete on production Javelins and, as I have explained earlier, there were always problems to be resolved on aircraft in service. But all this would not keep a major aircraft company with all the design, development and research activities in being. So what was to happen?

Civilian aircraft companies could turn their hands to developments in the emerging and fast growing civil airliner business, which, with one or two exceptions, had always been a private enterprise business. But Gloster's had always been a military aircraft business and relied heavily on defence contracts. On the other hand, it was the defence business that drove major advances in aviation technology. Without that spur, there would be a slow down. But what could Gloster's do? The finance involved in a private venture in military aviation put such a venture out of the question. Gloster's was, of course, part of a major group – Hawker Siddely Aviation Ltd – with many other interests and no doubt the future was already being discussed at Board level.

But, meanwhile, at Gloster's, what was to be done? Within the Engineering Research Department, as has been described, many developments and new innovations had taken place and thought was given as to how this could be turned to advantage. It was thought that some of the developments that had taken place could be further developed for commercial use. The pitch stabiliser, for example, was essentially an electro-hydraulic servo system. Were there possible applications in the machine tool industry? A great deal of work had been carried out on cabin air conditioning and temperature control systems. Could there be possibilities in systems for civilian aircraft, or even for domestic use? And, of course, there was the fuel/no air valve, in production for the Javelin, and the refuelling valve. Were there applications for these with other aircraft manufacturers? And the list went on.

In other areas of the company people were hard at work thinking of how to keep the company going and to retain the formidable team that had built up over the years. The aerodynamicists dreamed up a harvester that worked by air flow driving the harvested material up to storage. This was produced and, I believe, was in use for many years. Thought was also given to air drying systems for harvested crops. As Javelin production came to the end of the run, with no further orders, a local fire engine company was taken over and the factory space where aircraft used to be assembled became the assembly shop for fire engines. Not so incongruous as might be thought. Specialised fire engines and equipment are an essential feature of any airport.

Back at the Research Department ideas were crystallising and in due course I made a specific proposal to the Board of Directors that we become a commercial products division of the company, with the objective of exploiting the many developments within the department for general commercial use. Clearly, this was going to need financial support until products could be launched and sufficient sales generated to enable the division to be self-supporting. The proposal was supported by Mr H. B. Burroughs, who was then managing director of Gloster's as well as being chairman of Hawker Siddeley Group. It was also strongly supported by E. W. (Ted) Shambrook, company secretary.

It is to the everlasting credit of such people that the proposal was accepted and the new division was formally launched. It was named the Gloster Technical Developments Division, known as TDD for short, and kept things going for a while. It should be remembered that the Engineering Research Department had, by that time, grown into a substantial operation, all of it necessary to support the continual development, investigations, design support and, indeed, all the engineering work that is necessary to be in the business of modern military aircraft design and development. And, of course, we were not alone. There was also a Structural Engineering Department and a Flight Engineering Department all springing from the original Research Department.

Within engineering research, we now had large sections covering electrical and electronic, hydraulics and flying controls, air conditioning and fuel systems plus a substantial and very well equipped machine shop and workshop capable of producing almost anything. With, of course, full back up of office and secretarial staff. A total of all sections amounting to 270 people. So, we set about turning our developments and ideas into commercial products and finding a market. As part of the process of keeping things going, I made use of contacts that we had established with a company specialising in aviation refuelling equipment, as well as a range of commercial petrol pumps. They had more orders for their refuelling equipment than their production department could cope with. At the same time we were looking for work to keep the workshop and machine shop busy. So, we did a deal and successfully produced some of the Avery Hardoll range. We developed a complete production assembly line dedicated to producing Avery Hardoll Refuelling couplings. This was to be of great significance for myself personally later on.

In the whole of this transition period and, indeed, throughout the history of TDD, I cannot speak too highly of the enthusiasm and dedication of every one of the 270 people working there. And this was not just because they were looking out for their jobs. This was true dedication, enthusiasm and loyalty of everyone involved, from the shop floor upwards.

The list of products and equipment that was being developed and produced for the commercial market is impressive.

The start of it all was the pitch stabiliser for the Javelin, already referred to. (See p82). From this sprang a number of other electro-hydraulic devices. A need for accurate measurement of hydraulic flow when running tests on the aircraft led to the development of a unique, high pressure flow-meter with remote read-out. All these and many more soon led to an extensive range of products with commercial application, many driven by pressing needs from industry. An article in the magazine '*Machinery*' dated 12 November 1958 headed 'Gloster Control and Measuring Equipment' listed several products. Developments of the Electo-hydraulic servo-valve, as used in the pitch stabiliser, were described adapted to control the slide or cutter head on a machine tool for example. Mention was also made of the flow-meter mentioned above and a full range of force transducers and flow switches. The article went on to describe a profile indicator being produced, based on an original design from RAE Farnborough, that was capable of detecting changes in profile of as little as 0.000014 inch. Impressive by any standards and so the list went on.

The Hawker Siddeley Review of September 1958 carried an article headed 'Team with Talent'. Apart from some flattering comments about myself, this was a good summary of what TDD was all about. Some extracts are given now:

A man walked up to the Gloster section of the Hawker Siddeley Group stand at the Farnborough Show of 1956 and started to talk about some of the exhibits. It was apparent that his visit was the beginning of complete justification for Gloster's decision to supply, through their new Technical Developments Division, not only aircraft components, but pneumatic, electric, hydraulic and electro-hydraulic equipment for use in industry generally.

The turning point in the Technical Developments Division's affairs and the event which proved that the new department could compete in the open market and, what is more, produce a prototype in a remarkably short time came in May 1957.

Because of security only a skirting reference can be made to the actual circumstances; but it involved a requirement for an electro-hydraulic servo for the 'Javelin'. Mr E. W. Absolon, the chief engineer, created a team for this project and the outcome was that the prototype – in the basic form that was required – was put up within three months. The servo system completely met the bill, but – parallel with its technical qualities – it proved that the new organisation was able to compete keenly in the open market on design, price and delivery.

The speed with which the Javelin equipment had been produced has characterised the work of the new division since its formation. Within three months of the first Farnborough Show at which they exhibited, the first twenty micro-flow switches had been delivered to a machine tool manufacturer.

Development, output, and originality accelerated at such a rate from this period that it is impossible to mention all the Division's products in one article. One of the earlier products that epitomised the fresh thinking which is brought to bear by this youthful, eager organisation is the high pressure flow meter. With so much heavy machinery in industry operated by oil pressure, there was considerable interest in measuring the rate of flow of oil at pressures; but there were few firms in the world which could supply a meter to do this cheaply and accurately over a wide pressure range. Gloster TDD soon produced a flow meter that met all the requirements and the first batch of these meters went to HML (Engineering) for use on their aircraft servicing trolleys, trolleys from which the hydraulic systems on aircraft are checked during maintenance.

TDD have already produced a comprehensive range of pneumatic, reducing and hydraulic valves, together with aircraft ventilation systems and electrical apparatus, but one of their dominant interests for some time has been air data equipment... Quite apart from space (needed for the quantities of instruments now in use), the pilots job primarily is to fly his aeroplane and this becomes increasingly difficult if he has to correlate all the instrument readings in order to tell what is happening to the mass of equipment he is flying... With this in mind, the Gloster division is giving a considerable amount of its development time to air data computation and several units are at an advanced stage.

And so it goes on, finishing with...

Looking at the brochures and leaflets describing the range of TDD's products, it seems almost impossible that so much has been marketed in the space of two years. The solution lies in the speed in which the Gloster organisation gives concrete form to an idea and, underlying this, the quite refreshing enthusiasm of what is, in the main, a young team. This is no tongue-in-cheek phrase – the atmosphere is noticeable as soon as one walks in the door. It is a reflection of the creative intelligence of the chief engineer, Mr Absolon, who is very much a working member if the team. And it's the sort of atmosphere in which success flourishes.

This article spoke of the Pitch Stabiliser being developed within TDD, but I think, in fact, most of the work was done while we were still the Engineering Research Department and I was Chief of Engineering Research. The work was carried on into the newly formed Technical Developments Division, which was, in effect, the original Engineering Research Department.

As mentioned in the article, a display stand was organised at the SBAC at Farnborough, with an impressive array of the TDD products. (see photograph in plates)

So, everything was riding high and the future looked good for us, although the aircraft side of Gloster's business was in the doldrums. Several other ventures were in progress within the company. The aerodynamicists had come up with a design for a harvester that worked by drawing up the harvested material by aerodynamic flow. This looked like being successful and was to be produced within the aircraft production department. Another venture was into fire engines. A fire engine manufacturer, Alfred Miles, had been given space within the original flight test hangars on the other side of the airfield and they were then taken over by Gloster's and housed within the original aircraft production department. So it was all looking good for a continuing business at Gloster's, with various enterprises in progress, of which TDD was, of course a significant part.

And, of course, as mentioned earlier, we had established our capability, with the Avery Hardoll couplings, to manage a successful production line.

And then things began to change. We didn't know it, but the end was beginning. I received a telephone call from Hawker Siddeley Group head office in London. At that time, Sir Arnold Hall was Technical Director of the group. Sir Arnold came into fame when he was at the Royal Aircraft Establishment at Farnborough. He investigated and found the reason for the Comet disasters. Several aircraft were lost by exploding and disintegrating when climbing to cruising altitude after take-off. There was heavy loss of life. Sir Arnold designed and built a test rig that was able to simulate the conditions experienced, using a production Comet fuselage. Repeated tests eventually showed that the fundamental cause of the disaster was fatigue failure of the fuselage at a stress concentration point around the cabin windows. And now Sir Arnold wished to see me, in London at Group Head Office. An appointment was made and I travelled up, wondering what I was going to hear.

Sir Arnold was very pleasant and asked me all about TDD and how things were going. I gave him an update on our various activities. He had heard, of course, all about the Pitch Stabiliser and how that had been proved successful in flight trials. He then proceeded to give me some information, in strict confidence. I was not to be allowed to communicate this to anyone else, not even the Gloster directors.

Gloster Aircraft Company was to be closed, finished, to cease trading. There was not enough future for military aircraft and Gloster's were not in the civil aviation business, never had been, and were certainly not in the position now to venture into that area. My first thought was, of course, what about my division, what about those 270 people that have worked so hard to put us where we are. But I kept that to myself and waited for further enlightenment.

Sir Arnold went on to say that they (the group) were impressed with what had been achieved by my division and wanted to keep that part of Gloster's going. But there were similar activities taking place in other group companies. What the group now wanted was for me to visit all the other group companies, see what was going on and then make a report to the board on my recommendation as to what should be done with TDD, knowing that Gloster's was to cease trading. With hindsight, that put me in an almost impossible position. I had to go around the other group companies that were diversifying in to commercial ventures similar to Gloster TDD that I had started and was now running. I had to make a recommendation as to which other venture, or ventures, could be merged to advantage with TDD. I was privy to the knowledge that Gloster's was to be closed, but I was not allowed to discuss, or even reveal, that knowledge to the very people at Gloster's who had supported and encouraged me in the venture of TDD. Impossible!

But I then set about making appointments and visiting the other group companies. The other group venture that made entire sense to me was at Armstrong Whitworth in Coventry. Their commercial venture was Armstrong Whitworth Equipment (AWE) and it was run by the son of one of the company directors. I wrote a report and recommended that TDD and AWE merge. This was agreed and the director's son that ran AWE was made my deputy and was based at Gloster. In effect, my division was sold to Armstrong Whitworth, but I remained in charge at Gloster and AWE remained at Coventry.

The Gloster directors who had supported me were devastated. And I was still not allowed to tell them that Gloster's was to close and there was no alternative. Another defining moment in my life, almost as bad as Bill Waterton cornering me in that office at Boscombe Down with the challenge 'Is this thing safe to fly?' Lifetime memories are made of this.

Chapter 11

The End of an Era

Work continued as part of Armstrong Whitworth, but my division was never the same. We were, in effect, Armstrong Whitworth Equipment and something in the whole organisation died. The spirit that had been so vibrant and had kept everything going had gone. At that time I had some wonderful people working for me and the management team that had been built up consisted of a Sales Manager, a Chief Electrical Engineer, a Works Manager, a Fuel Systems Engineer and an excellent secretary and PA for me. We had an Electronics Lab., an Electrical Systems Lab., a Fuel Management Department, Hydraulics Engineering Department and, last but by no means least, a magnificent workshop, with machine shop, fabrication and welding, assembly, etc.

Altogether I had 270 people working for me and I was so proud of them all. I used to boast that they would have done anything for the division and myself. I had excellent relations with the Trade Unions and they were part of the whole team effort. We continued to try and use the aviation technology, learnt the hard way, into commercial products that would keep everything going. The important thing to us was not to let the hard won technology of the aircraft development die. It was too important and there was a world out there awaiting new development and technology to make life better for all. Quite apart from all that, it was a livelihood for all those people that had given so much of their lives to development and manufacture of the aircraft and all the associated systems. Earlier, in the Gloster TDD days, I had several battles with the Gloster directors over conditions and pay for the men working for me. Of course, they had to take into account the whole workforce at Gloster, amounting to some 5,000 and I respected that. But it didn't stop me from fighting for my corner.

And then it began to change. Slowly, almost unnoticed at first, but change it did. I trusted completely in the new arrangements, at least I thought I did, and worked together with my new deputy. It was difficult, because he obviously had other responsibilities, of which I was not a part. Then I began to receive critical reports from the director at Armstrong Whitworth. For example, I was criticised for my handling of the Trade Unions. That hurt me deeply. As I have said, I had excellent relations with the Trade Unions and we never had any trouble in that direction. Yes, of course, we had our differences from time to time, but they were always resolved to everyone's satisfaction. I like to think that we had a happy ship.

As a side issue, it might be worth recording an incident back in the Gloster Aircraft days concerning Trade Union handling that always impressed me. There was a factory shop steward who was a thorn in the side of management because he was always complaining about the state of the canteen. No works canteen can please everyone, by the very nature of the task of feeding up to 5,000 people every day, but there were problems that, perhaps, should not have been there. So what did the Gloster management do? They offered the job of canteen manager to that troublesome shop steward. End of story. No more complaints and the canteen improved dramatically. Perhaps a lesson for some present day problems?

Going back to the division and the changes, slowly, almost imperceptibly taking place, things began to accelerate. My deputy was moving around amongst the laboratories and staff. I had received another critical report from Coventry and rumours must have been circulating amongst the staff. I accidentally overheard a conversation between my deputy and one of the senior engineers. I heard my engineer, who had always been so loyal to me and the division, say, 'But he is the boss after all.' I don't know what preceded that, but I heard my deputy say, 'But he asked for it.' So then I realised that things were going on behind my back and it dawned on me that information was being fed back to Coventry without my knowledge. I trusted and I was let down. It culminated in my receiving a damning report from Coventry, accusing me of, in effect, total mismanagement and quoting all sorts of figures that were completely misleading. I responded with a lengthy document, refuting some of the statements and quoting the facts as I saw it. The document I received was based on many false assumptions as I saw it.

At the same time I began to realise that the future was not looking too good for me. The writing was starting to appear on the wall. I had developed good relations with Avery Hardoll, whose couplings we were manufacturing and I began to wonder about alternative employment. I had got to know and respect their Director/Commercial Manager (D/CM) and he let it be known that, following some retirements, he was about to reorganise the company management and split the Design Department in to two. There would be a Chief Designer (Industrial Equipment) and a Chief Designer (Garage Equipment). At that time the company had a range of garage petrol pumps and a range of industrial equipment, a major part of which was the aviation refuelling coupling. The managing director was close to retirement and it was pretty obvious that their D/CM would become the managing director.

The post of Chief Designer (Industrial Equipment) was about to be advertised and it was suggested that I might like to apply. This seemed like an ordained opportunity to get out of what seemed like an increasingly difficult and pessimistic situation in which I found myself, although it carried less responsibility and was further away.

And more than that, things were happening within my division, behind my back. I was going to get in to a conflict of personalities. I was going to have to accept that my trust in others was misplaced and I have never been able to cope with that situation. I had always trusted people and it looked as though that trust was misplaced. More than that perhaps, all those wonderful people that worked for me, what was to happen to them?

So I applied for the post. I was invited to an interview, which seemed to go well. I was told that in the longer term the two design departments may be combined and there would probably be a post of Technical Manager. Also, the industrial side of the company would shortly move to Havant on the south coast, and eventually the whole company would move from the present location in Chessington. So, I awaited to hear the result of the interview.

As it turned out, the whole thing was accelerated for me. There was no direct reply to my response to the report from Coventry that had upset me so much, but a few days later I received a memo saying, 'Come and report to my office at 11.00am tomorrow. I have to tell you that it may not be very pleasant.' The office was in Coventry at Armstrong Whitworth Head Office. So, I drove up to Coventry, wondering of course, what was in store. I knew it would probably be unpleasant. Perhaps a severe reprimand over my response to the critical (and in my view unjustified report) but nothing could have prepared me for what happened. I reported to the director concerned at precisely 11.00am. There was no greeting, nothing, he just said.

'Straight from the shoulder, you are no longer a member of this company. Goodbye.' That was it. No explanation, nothing. More words that one remembers for the rest of life, along with Bill Waterton's question, 'Is this thing safe to fly?' and, 'be it on your head.' And now, 'You are no longer a member of this company.'

I drove back to Gloster's in a daze. I couldn't believe it would happen just like that. I knew that things were going wrong, but I did not expect that sort of treatment. It was only too obvious that things had been going on behind my back. Why, oh why did I trust? And what about all those wonderful people that worked for me? What changes were afoot for them? And would it have made any difference anyway? Is this what was planned from the start of the take over when my deputy was appointed? I will never know.

When I got back all the formalities of discharge were put in place. The paperwork and formal notice of termination of employment. My first step was to telephone Avery Hardoll and ask to speak to the director that had interviewed me. I said that there had been a development and could I please come up and see him straight away? I did not say what it was about. I was concerned that when I informed him that I had, effectively, been discharged it would adversely affect my application. He said straight away, yes certainly, come up. I think it was set for the next day, or even perhaps later the same day. Anyway, I drove up and presented myself. I told him what had happened and said that I was concerned that it would affect my application. I shall always remember his answer.

'Don't worry,' he said, 'probably a good thing. We are going to offer you the job anyway.' So, that was it. My days in the aircraft industry were over and I was to start again. I was to leave the industry that I loved. My direct association with aircraft, that had driven me for so long, was at an end. But, thankfully, not quite. Avery Hardoll were involved in aviation to an extent, with refuelling couplings and bulk flow meters used in aircraft fuelling dispensers. So who knows what the future may bring? More than that, perhaps, I was to work for someone that I had found very likeable on first impressions. As described in the next chapter, I came to like him more and found that I could work very happily for him. I came to trust him and that trust was never betrayed. His name was Ron Mitchell, sadly no longer with us, but I shall be eternally grateful for my time working for him.

So, that was it. When I got back to Gloster's I told all my management team what had happened and that I was leaving on the date that had been set. The word quickly spread of course and arrangements were made to say farewell. My deputy that was to take over kept out of it. In fact, if memory serves me correctly, he returned to Coventry until I had finally left. The

Leaving Stroud for new post

MR. E. W. ABSOLON, of Stroud, and manager of Armstrong Whitworth Equipment, formerly the Technical Developments Division of GAC, is leaving to become chief design engineer with Avery Hardoll's of Kingston, manufacturers of garage and industrial equipment.

Mr Absolon, who is 55, joined GAC in 1946 and, with the exception of two years with Dowty's, has been at Brockworth the whole time.

Former chief engineer of the Technical Developments project, he was appointed manager last May He takes up his new post in the new year.

Married, with two children, his home is at Wood Close, Summer-st., Stroud. He is chairman of the Stroud Parish Church finance committee, and vice-chairman of the St. Alban's Church committee.

In our picture Mr. Absolon taps the barometer which was presented to him, together with a wristlet watch, by members of the staff and works employees at Armstrong Whitworth Equipment Ltd.

Farewell, the end of an era.

~ AWA AFFAIRS ~ June 1959

A.W.A. TAKES OVER GLOSTER T.D.D.

ON JUNE 1 Sir W. G. Armstrong Whitworth Aircraft Ltd. took over the Technical Development Division of Gloster Aircraft Company. The move brings together our own rapidly expanding commercial electronics department at A.W.A. and a Gloster division which is working in similar fields and breaking into new markets.

Gloster T.D.D. will continue to manufacture their existing range of products, which includes various forms of valves, hydraulic and electronic equipment, and will also assist in the production of items from A.W.A's. commercial electronic department.

The takeover will bring together two departments producing a complementary range of equipment with a wide application in the fields of instrumentation, automation and radio communication as well as aircraft and guided missile systems as a whole.

Mr. E. W. Absolon, who has been chief engineer at T.D.D., has been appointed manager of the new division. Mr. A. E. Martin, who has been in charge of A.W.A. Commercial Electronics Department, will move to Gloucester as deputy Divisional Manager.

Mr. E. W. Absolon.   Mr. A. E. Martin.

The sales and marketing of products from both the Gloucester and Coventry factories will be the responsibility of Gloster T.D.D. under the T.D.D. Sales Director, Mr. P. Emmett.

The new division will be known as the Gloster Technical Development Division of Sir. W. G. Armstrong Whitworth Aircraft Ltd.

---

response from my team was overwhelming. My management team insisted on taking me out for an evening meal. They would not let me do anything. I was to be collected and returned. I could have as many drinks as I liked! All the workers collected for gifts, of which I am so proud. They gave me a Rolex watch, which I have worn every day to this day and which I intend to wear for the rest of my life. It is inscribed:

"Presented to Mr E W Absolon by Gloster TDD. November 1959"

Note, Gloster TDD not Armstrong Whitworth Equipment. I am particularly proud of a separate presentation from the Trade Union. A barometer that has pride of place in the hall of our house. Shown in the photograph, I am tapping it with great pride, as I still do every night.

Sometime after that, I did return to the Gloster site, for some reason that I have long since forgotten. With hindsight I rather wish that I hadn't. What was once a great aircraft factory producing many superb aircraft, particularly in our time of greatest need during the war, was now a trading estate. The birth place and home of the very first jet powered aircraft, the E1/44 with the original Whittle jet engine. The twin jet Meteor in all its many variants. The only aircraft that could catch the German V1 flying bomb and bring it down. The clever part was that the point of interception could be chosen, to some extent, so that hopefully the bomb would land and explode in an area without houses.

Another Meteor at one time held the world air speed record. It was specially prepared and flown by Group Captain Donaldson. A remarkable aircraft, from a design team headed by J. C. Carter.

And then the Javelin, on which I and many others spent so much time and effort. The Javelin never achieved the glamour and status of the Meteor. Not liked by many, rather cumbersome and ugly looking by some standards. But it was designed to do a job, to a specification issued by the Ministry of Defence and it performed that job to the specification.

And now, what was left? I wandered around the site. The runway, from which all these aircraft, when in production, had taken off for their first flight. That first flight always watched by all the workers with great pride. They would take a few minutes off, with full management tolerance and understanding, to see the thing that they had created take to the skies. That runway, historic in its significance, now covered in grass and neglected, with no indication of the never-to-be-forgotten events that happened there.

And the buildings, some occupied, many neglected. Windows broken, covered in dust. The hangars, once the home of these great aircraft, now consigned to the scrap heap. Grass was now growing on the roofs, just awaiting final destruction to make way for some new, modern, building to suit the new usage.

And then, the final wound to pride. I wandered in to what was originally the assembly shop, where all the production aircraft were finally put together and prepared for flight. What was once that wonderful array of rows of beautiful flying machines being lovingly finished was now a production line of road tankers. The objects that gave such pride and joy to all those that worked there, had given way to mundane, ordinary looking road tankers with no soul. In my imagination I could still hear the sound of rivet guns and all the familiar sounds of an aircraft production line. A production line, where finally, all the thousands of separate items that made the design came together and became this flying machine. Yes, still a machine, but a machine with a soul like no other. A machine that could soar in to the air at will, climb away, perform unheard of manoeuvres at breathtaking speed, roll, loop, dive and fly away to distant destinations at speeds unheard of just a few years ago. More than that, machines equipped to defend our country against enemy attack. That could climb, intercept an intruder. That was armed with the very latest in weapon technology, destined for pilots in the Royal Air Force that were trained in their use.

All this went through my mind in what was probably seconds. And now this. A line of industrial road tankers, fit for their own purpose, necessary for our needs, but never the same. Never could arise the same pride and passion, pride to be a part of the whole scene of developing aviation.

Of course, there were other aircraft factories in production with some military aircraft and the emerging civil aviation industry, but it would never be the same. With the emergence of computers and ever larger and more complex aircraft, complex and large design teams were necessary. The individuality that made life so exciting and satisfying was going, never to return.

Truly the end of an era, never to be equalled. Farewell.

Chapter 12

After Gloster's

So, after the heartbreak of leaving my beloved division that I had spent so long building up, and after finally saying goodbye to all those marvellous people that had worked for me, I took up my new job at Avery Hardoll, who, at that time were based at Chessington, but, as said earlier, the production of industrial equipment had moved to a new factory on an industrial estate at Havant, Hampshire. I joined as Chief Designer, Industrial Equipment. Every management position in the company was known by initials – hence I was CDIE. There was also a Chief Designer Garage Equipment, CDGE and so on. The interest for me in particular in the industrial equipment range was a bulk flow-meter, used on aircraft refuelling vehicles at the airports, as well as industrial applications, together with an aviation refuelling nozzle that connects to the aircraft being refuelled, hydrant pit valves and various accessories.

For those not familiar with the aviation refuelling process, there are two methods of refuelling an aircraft. The first is a refuelling tanker that is filled at a remote storage area and can then travel around the airfield and refuel waiting aircraft. These are used mainly on the smaller airfields where traffic density is not too great and there is room for the refuelling tanker to operate between aircraft. Also, the tanker can carry sufficient fuel to fill the aircraft in one operation.

The second is a hydrant system. These exist on the larger airfields, dealing with much larger aircraft. A jumbo jet, for example, requires something like 29,000 gallons for a transatlantic flight. The hydrant system is located under the ground and can distribute fuel to the designated areas for aircraft loading/unloading. The pipelines terminate in individual hydrant pits, located at the strategic points.

Because there are often two types of aviation fuel on any one airfield, jet fuel and aviation gasoline, great care has to be taken to keep them separate and to prevent the wrong fuel being loaded into an aircraft. Generally speaking, light aircraft and older aircraft types are driven by piston type engines and use gasoline. Aviation gasoline is similar to petrol used in the average motor car, but to higher specification and subject to stringent quality control. The vast majority of commercial, passenger carrying, aircraft are jet engine driven and use aviation turbine fuel, or more commonly known as jet fuel. Jet fuel is essentially kerosene and, like aviation gasoline is produced and stored to high quality standards. The modern jet engine requires fuel produced accurately to specification and quality standards. In particular it must not contain water. Kerosene is basically hydroscopic. That is to say it easily absorbs water.

Therefore hydrant dispensers and refuelling tankers have to be fitted with filter/water separators to ensure that no water or contamination can enter the aircraft. Furthermore, it is, of course, absolutely essential that the aircraft is not fuelled with the wrong fuel. There have been cases of an accident caused by this happening. In one classic instance, a piston engined aircraft was fuelled with jet fuel in error. There was sufficient gasoline in the carburetors and pipework for the aircraft to get airborne, but shortly afterwards jet fuel came through and both engines stalled. The aircraft ditched in the sea.

Avery Hardoll manufactured an aviation refuelling nozzle, together with the associated coupling fitted to the aircraft. Whether from a hydrant dispenser or a refuelling tanker, the nozzle and adaptor are the same. To deal with the problem of possible wrong fuelling, the nozzle and aircraft adaptor are keyed such that a mis-connection cannot be made. The aircraft adaptor is keyed in accordance with the aircraft type to which it is fitted (jet fuel or gasoline) and the dispenser nozzle keyed accordingly. Therefore it is impossible to connect the wrong fuel to the aircraft. Simple. But not quite… One of the early problems that I had to deal with was a case of a refuelling nozzle not connecting correctly.

All refuelling nozzles are designed with an interlock, such that it is not possible to open the nozzle and initiate fuel flow unless the nozzle is correctly connected to the aircraft and sealed. In this case it was possible to achieve the apparent impossible. It was possible to have the nozzle apparently connected, open the valve and initiate flow, only to find that connection had not been properly made, the nozzle not sealed. Result – aviation fuel flowing out of the connection at pressure and spewing fuel everywhere. Panic! But quickly disconnected, fire engines on scene in case of ignition and everything cleared up. It may not seem a major problem, but in modern commercial passenger carrying operations, turn around at the airport is critical. Any commercial aircraft is only earning money when flying. Any delay is totally un-acceptable from an operational viewpoint, apart from the anger and frustration of passengers and congestion at the airport terminal.

At one time, the possibility of refuelling the aircraft with the wrong fuel was a real worry.

There is now, however, a constant and great awareness of the problem and at all airports there are strict precautions to prevent any possibility of mis-fuelling. The problem was always more of a worry at the smaller airports where there would be a higher proportion of smaller, piston engined aircraft and more refuelling taking place with gasoline. At the larger airports the proportion of jet aircraft is very much higher and only the small piston engined aircraft would be refuelled by tanker, all the jet fuel coming from a hydrant system. Furthermore, light aircraft operations and refuelling would be entirely separate from the larger, jet engined, passenger carrying aircraft.

Having said that, in later years, after Avery Hardoll, I was asked to carry out a survey of the fuelling systems at one or two of the smaller airfields, where all fuelling was by tanker. There was no hydrant system. In one case in particular I was alarmed at the closeness of the different fuelling facilities and what seemed to me to be a real risk of wrong fuelling. I asked about it and said I was concerned. The answer? "Oh, that's not a problem. Our tanker driver has been here years, he knows all the aircraft and which fuel they take anyway." The classic situation for a human error mishap. It does happen.

Going back to the original problem, my investigation in the USA revealed that the problem was caused by wear of the selectivity slots on the refuelling nozzle. This enabled a partial connection to be made to the aircraft coupling, resulting in the spillage encountered. A classic case of the necessity for regular maintenance checks on anything to do with aircraft, no matter how inconsequential it may seem.

Another instance worth recording occurred at London Heathrow after the refuelling of a transatlantic aircraft before take-off. The oil company concerned always carried out a check of the refuelling equipment after use. This check included an examination of the refuelling nozzle. In this particular instance, an Avery Hardoll nozzle was fitted to the dispenser concerned. All refuelling nozzles have an inward vent valve fitted to prevent negative pressure in the refuelling hose should fuel be drawn back to the dispenser. The post-refuelling check on the equipment showed that the inward vent valve parts – a spring and valve – were missing. An immediate search was carried out, hopefully, to locate the missing parts, but without success. The possible conclusion was that the parts could have been drawn into the aircraft fuelling system. This was quite unacceptable and the airline concerned was immediately notified. Unfortunately, the aircraft had already left and was well on its way across the Atlantic, heading for New York. The airline decided that the aircraft should be diverted to the nearest diversion airport. This was in Greenland. Passengers and baggage had to be unloaded and, eventually, transferred to another aircraft to take them on to New York.

The aircraft fuel system was then completely dismantled in a search for the missing parts. Nothing was found. It was assumed that the missing parts were lost elsewhere and not found. The aircraft was cleared for service. It should be recorded that the oil company concerned and the operating airline took full responsibility and no liability was directed toward the coupling manufacturer, Avery Hardoll. This is because any piece of equipment for use in connection with the aircraft is subjected to rigorous testing by the operating company using it. If the test is passed, then the operating company accepts full responsibility for its use. Nevertheless, I initiated an immediate revised design to ensure that such an event could not happen again. If nothing else, this incident serves to illustrate the rigorous standards applied to anything connected with the operation of aircraft. Such standards and procedures are at the heart of the very high safety record of recognised civilian airlines, standards strictly enforced by the Air Registration Board and all other connected authorities.

Avery Hardoll also designed and manufactured refuelling hydrant system control valves mounted in the hydrant pit. These also included a fundamental, but very simple safety feature. A lanyard was attached to a quick closure feature of the hydrant control valve and kept close to the refuelling operator. In the event of a spillage, a quick pull on the lanyard would immediately close the valve and prevent any more leakage. It is interesting to note that amongst all the high tech equipment, a simple pull lanyard was a vital piece of safety equipment. Simple, but effective. A lesson for some present day highly complicated systems? It is interesting that in later life, with my own company, and acting in a consultancy capacity, I assisted with a patent application for a Hydrant Guard, a complicated system to prevent airfield vehicles from accidentally driving into the pit area while refuelling was in progress.

It is important to understand the rigorous safety standards applied to the refuelling procedure. It may seem simple to pump fuel into the aircraft before a flight, but there are many aspects that are critical. First of all, the time available, no aircraft is earning money while on the ground. There is great pressure to achieve a rapid turn around and get the aircraft back into the air. Passenger and baggage boarding is one item and refuelling the other. Furthermore, the quantity of fuel has to be precise for the planned flight. Enough to reach the planned destination plus a defined reserve to cover flying control delays at the destination and enough to reach a diversion airfield, should that become necessary. Diversion could be for a number of reasons, bad weather, security alarm, some fault in the aircraft system and so on. Modern civilian aircraft are extremely reliable and driven by computer, with all systems duplicated, or even triplicated, but a technical fault could occur prompting the captain to divert. Coming down to a lower altitude and taking off again will consume more fuel that cruising at altitude, the reason why cruising altitudes have become higher and higher over the years. The cost of fuel is a significant part of any airline operating costs.

An essential part of safety standards is the quality control of the fuel. It may be thought that a jet engine is more tolerant to variations in fuel that the conventional piston engine, petrol driven, but not so. Rigorous standards are applied to the production of jet fuel and the maintenance of specification standards. The control and maintenance of standards are usually in the hands of a professional organisation. In our case, the Energy Institute, will have a committee of professional people, experienced in the art and totally dedicated to safety. When jet fuel is produced by the oil company concerned it will, of course, be subjected to all the necessary controls to meet the standard before being transported to the airfield. Transport itself is a major issue and the quantities involved are enormous. As mentioned earlier, a jumbo jet will typically take on board around 29,000 gallons for a transatlantic flight. This means vast storage facilities at the airport and a continuous delivery system, by road transport at the smaller airports, but by pipeline at the larger airports.

Gatwick, for example, is fed by pipeline from the main storage terminal at Hamble, on the Southampton Water, where it is fed by sea tanker amongst other transport.

So, in spite of all the complex and rigorous application of safety standards and procedures at the production end, procedures also have to be applied when delivering to the aircraft. These are mainly bulk accuracy, filtration and, most important, water content. All petroleum based products are, by their very nature, hydroscopic and will pick up water in transit. Water is anathema to any engine, including jet engines, when cruising at high altitude, because of the danger of freezing and ice particles blocking the filters, causing fuel starvation to the engines.

Bulk accuracy is important for two reasons. The flight crew will call for a precise quantity of fuel, based on the flight plan, weather conditions, etc. Also, fuel is sold to the airline, based on the meter readings on the fuel dispenser, whether a vehicle bulk tanker dispenser or a hydrant dispenser. Therefore the meter dispensing the fuel has to be to weights and measures standards in the country concerned.

So, it can be seen that whether by hydrant or a mobile fuelling tanker, pumping fuel into the aircraft is not, by any standards, a simple matter. It requires absolute precision in all aspects, summed up by quantity and quality. Every piece of dispensing equipment, on any airfield, large or small, anywhere in the world has to conform to rigorous standards. As with anything to do with flying, safety is paramount and takes priority over everything.

In spite of all the standards and procedures, things do sometimes arise that have not been foreseen and have to be dealt with. A classic case was that of a bacteria that developed and learnt how to live and reproduce in an aircraft jet fuel tank. It was called Gladispora Sputae and the problem was that it produced a jelly substance that gradually spread in the tank and could cause major problems with filter blockage. The solution was to inject a biocide into the fuel and also to be very strict on preventing water in the fuel, which assisted reproduction of the bacteria. In the meanwhile, this triggered a major maintenance operation. All aircraft had to be checked and, where necessary, tanks cleaned out. On a modern complex aircraft this is not as simple as it sounds.

In all these situations we learn and apply corrective action, but sometimes, unfortunately, not until a major problem has become apparent. One cannot help asking – do we learn as quickly as even the most primitive form of life on earth – a basic bacteria that discovers how to make use of our modern technology to reproduce?

All of these problems and developments in the aviation scene were interesting and exciting to me in particular, but, of course, I was now Technical Manager for the company and therefore technically responsible for the whole range of products of the company. Obviously, anything remotely connected to aviation were the things closest to my heart, but I found very quickly that garage equipment, the other branch of the company's activity, also had its technical attraction.

The garage petrol pump may not look anything much, but it does have to conform to strict weights and measures standards. It is used to dispense petrol to the public and the cost display on the pump is what the customer is asked to pay. Originally, the first generation of petrol pumps just showed a quantity. The pump was operated by an attendant who noted the quantity and then charged the customer accordingly, exactly the same as buying a quantity of any product in a shop. Go into the grocers and either pick up, or ask for, a quantity of, for example, potatoes, and the shop assistant will weigh and charge according to the published price per unit weight. Shops have progressed (some think unfortunately) to supermarkets where, very often, the product is pre-packed and priced. At the check-out payment is made accordingly with no other process. No more weighing or calculation.

The same process has taken place in petrol dispensing equipment. The first development was to incorporate a price computer in the pump. The operator can set the price per unit volume at the pump and the pump automatically displays the total computed price for the customer to pay. Originally, this was a simple mechanical computer, rather like the very early desk calculating machines used in offices, later superseded by electronics. But before that another factor intruded. Originally petrol was petrol and all cars used the same fuel. But the car industry began to develop technically, as with all industries. All industries are competitive, by their very nature. Any one industry will have competition and will wish to stay ahead of their competitors and, if possible, even increase their share of the market. This is the very nature of our democratic society, totally dependent on private enterprise.

So, the individual car manufacturers began to look for selling features. More power, more acceleration, more speed. This resulted in engine development with higher compression ratios and higher RPM (revs per minute) to give more power for a given weight and size. Critically important in the design of a motor car is to have customer appeal. Weight is, of course, especially important in achieving high acceleration, a feature much sought after until very recently, when economy and long life has become more important to many.

The feature that we are particularly interested in is compression ratio. For the non-technical reader, this is basically, the ratio of total swept cylinder volume divided by the volume remaining with the piston at the top of the stroke. For example, if the total cylinder volume is 400cc and the volume left with the piston at the top of its stroke is 50cc, then the compression ratio will be eight. For a given cylinder capacity, within limits, a higher compression ratio will give a higher power output. This is because a given unit volume of fuel has a specific calorific value, depending on the specification and make-up of the fuel and to some extent is dependant on the quality of the original crude oil from which the petrol is refined. The energy in the fuel (calorific value) is released by ignition under pressure. Some of this energy powers the engine. The remainder disappears as heat down the exhaust pipe. Typically, in a motor car, only about forty per cent is used in the engine, sixty per cent is wasted to exhaust heat.

It so happens that the higher the compression ratio on ignition (i.e. the higher pressure of the petrol/air mixture on ignition) the higher the efficiency of the engine. Which means, in turn, that more of the fuel energy is converted to power and less disappears down the exhaust pipe to the earth's atmosphere. But if higher compression is used on normal, standard motor petrol, "knocking" occurs, which is plainly audible. "Knocking" is, in effect, pre-ignition of the fuel before the spark plug operates, which results in a poor engine performance and defeats the object. To recognise this phenomena, the ability of a given grade of fuel to accept a higher compression ratio without pre-ignition is designated by a number, known as the Octane number. The higher the number, the higher compression ratio that can be used and therefore the higher the efficiency of the engine. But, of course, a more refined fuel, with higher octane rating, costs more to produce and therefore the price at the pump is higher.

Here was an opportunity for the oil companies to be competitive and, in consequence, for the petrol pump manufacturing companies to design and offer equipment suited to the market at that time. The result was a garage forecourt dispensing pump that could offer up to five different grades of petrol, that is with five different octane ratings. This meant up to five different prices and up to five different total cost displays. This was known as a Blend Pump, because it produced the grades on offer by blending in the correct ratio from two grades of petrol delivered to the garage forecourt, one with a high octane rating and the other at the low end. At the same time the pump had to compute the price to be paid. This meant a device that could measure quantity and compute price for the blend selected. This was before the days of electronics on the forecourt, so quite a challenge!

At that time there was a Petrol Pump Manufacturer's Association (PPMA) and we had regular meetings. There was only one other petrol pump company of significance at the time, the Beck Meter and Pump Company and we formed a liaison with them, particularly over this question of the oil companies requirement for a blend pump on the forecourt. It quickly became apparent that there was a worldwide patent in force by the Wayne Tank and Pump Co. of the USA. Everybody else who wanted to introduce a blend pump had signed up with Wayne and taken a license, which, of course, cost in a license fee.

I took a long look at the Wayne patent and was determined to find a way round it. Eventually a design was evolved that, in the opinion of our patent agent, would not infringe the Wayne patent. My design team quickly set to work and produced a detailed design ready for production. Prototype trials were conducted and were successful, so the pump was produced and installed on garage forecourts.

Then, another dramatic change in the market. Self service. This came about as a result of two pressures – one from the consumer and the other from the state of the garage forecourt business. Consumers were getting agitated about two aspects – the ever rising cost of petrol and, as increasingly busy people, especially on business, the time taken to fill up. Wait for an attendant, sit doing nothing while the attendant filled up, then having to go to the office to pay. The other was the state of the garage forecourt business in general. Garages used to be a place where repairs and servicing were carried out, with a labour force accordingly. Petrol was sold largely as a side issue. Gradually this changed. Servicing and repairs was a function largely controlled by the motor car industry and became a specialised aspect of the garage operation. This, in turn, drove a division of the garage business into two – specialised servicing and repair centres, largely supported by the motor car industry, and the petrol dispensing industry largely supported by the oil companies. The two establishments became quite separate entities.

We are concerned with the petrol dispensing business and, with the small sales margins on petrol and a highly competitive market, the cost of labour was a significant factor in trying to run a business at a profit.

So, the idea was born of minimising labour and getting the customer to do more of the work themselves. There were some early attempts to provide a remote read-out in the kiosk, but this was cumbersome and slow, leading to queues and impatience. The idea was born of using electronics to provide computing of price from volume dispensed with an instantaneous display in the kiosk. I formed an electronics section within the design department to explore and pursue an electronic self service system. This eventually resulted in a fully operational self service system that could be demonstrated to the oil companies. It was accepted and a trial system ordered and installed on a company owned site. The trials were successful and we were proud of the fact that we had demonstrated the very first electronic self service station in this country. (see photograph in plates)

The system was quickly taken up and resulted in the virtual elimination of the old style garage with petrol sales as an extra. What happened next is history and typical of the constant competitiveness in any retail market. With constant price cutting for any one forecourt to stay ahead of the competition, another sales outlet was desperately required to justify the cost of just one operator. So the idea of combining the fuel dispensing business with a retail outlet came into being and the garage forecourt changed its nature by becoming a retail shop. In many cases the retail sales were more significant and provided better margins and returns than petrol and diesel. And so it remains to this day.

With so much technology developing all the time, one is tempted to ponder – what next? The answer almost certainly will be the inevitable replacement of petrol and all oil based fuels with a new technology. Oil will run out within the next forty to fifty years and before then it will become extremely expensive. There is no argument about this. Yes. there are some undeveloped reserves, but they are difficult, expensive and risky (witness the disaster for BP in the Gulf of Mexico). And there are some alternatives, biofuel, methane, etc. But these will be in short supply and therefore expensive. Some are suitable for road transport, but not so far for aircraft propulsion. The most abundant source of energy in the world is solar power, but there is much to be done, both in development and politically before this can be available in a form suitable for aircraft propulsion.

This is an area of research and development that needs to be pursued with urgency. There are ideas, but not the subject of this book.

So, life continued at Avery Hardoll. With the support and help of the Managing Director, Ron Mitchell, who constantly inspired me and offered nothing but encouragement at all times, we developed further into industrial applications for electronics, particularly with metering systems. The Avery Hardoll bulkmeter, well established before my time, was still one of the best in the business and the demand grew for complete systems formed around this meter. I formed a Systems Engineering section to deal with the demand. A typical system would be at a road tanker loading depot, transporting petroleum product from bulk storage to retail garage outlets and airfields in the case of aviation fuel. Such systems were not as simple as might be imagined.

Tankers were monitored in and out of the depot and directed to the appropriate loading position A typical terminal might have several lanes for different product grades and each lane would have a number of loading stations with loading arms ready for top fill. The tankers were programmed by computer so that they could be loaded and directed to their destination with maximum efficiency of overall operation. The whole system would be displayed and monitored in a central control room, with remote read-out from the meters. An Avery Hardoll pre-set valve would be incorporated close to the meter so that the required volume to be loaded could be pre-set and controlled centrally.

The whole subject of loading tankers was another subject that we dealt with and came up with a solution. Traditionally, tankers were top loaded with a loading arm. This entailed the driver, or an operator, climbing to the top of the vehicle, opening a hatch and directing a loading arm, terminating in a piece of hose, into the open hatchway. This had all sorts of problems, not the least of which was the release of vapour to the atmosphere, with the obvious risks. There was one classic and tragic case that affected everybody deeply. A man lost his life. I think there had been a spillage, as well as vapour release. There was an obvious hazard and a tanker driver nearby thought that he ought to move his vehicle away. Unfortunately, this was to result in disaster. Starting up the engine caused a spark from the unshielded starter motor that set off an explosion and fire. The driver that had tried to help lost his life.

This and other factors brought about the requirement for bottom loading of vehicles through a closed, sealed, coupling that would not release vapour. In the case of a 'full tank' fill, this would require some form of top level control, so that without the need for an operator to be on top of the tank, flow would be stopped at the required level. There were conventional systems for controlling level in a tank available, consisting of a float operated valve at the top level, that cut off a pilot flow to the main filling valve causing it to close. But such a device seemed vulnerable in a road tanker, with road vibration and possible large disturbances, driving over bumps or sudden braking.

Our solution was Jet Able. (Jet operated Automatic Bottom Loading Equipment.) This consisted of a conventional foot valve in the bottom of the vehicle compartment. Conventionally, this would have been operated by a float valve in the top of the compartment that sensed top fluid level and operated a pilot flow circuit. In Jet Able the float operation was replaced by a jet of fluid jumping across a gap to a receiving orifice opposite. As long as the flow was not interrupted, pressure would be sensed in the receiving orifice, which through the pilot circuit would keep the main foot valve open. As soon as the jet flow was interrupted by rising fluid level in the tank, at the designed level, the receiving orifice pressure became dispersed and the foot valve closed. The device was proven to work very well and was soon in production.

Top loading, with all its hazards, became a thing of the past. Digressing slightly, one aspect of a top loading hazard that would not normally be seen is worth recording. I was asked, through our agent there, to go to South Africa to investigate a problem that had arisen on road tanker loading. I was taken to a loading depot where top loading of road tankers was taking place. I do not recall what the actual problem was, but I was surprised to see local men on top of the tanker while it was top loading, with the compartment lid open, of course. I asked what several men were doing on top of the tanker at once. Surely unnecessary? The answer in general terms was – don't ask! What was actually happening of course was that the men were sniffing the petroleum vapour, using it like a drug. It had been determined at that time that it was best to leave them alone and not interfere.

And so life continued. With the support of the Managing Director, Ron Mitchell (now laid to rest) I continued to build a technical team so that we could tackle any new market situation that arose and respond to forward requirements from the sales department. At that time, the whole team at Avery Hardoll appeared to be strong. In the technical department, we now had the normal drawing office, a Systems Engineering section, a Test and Development Department, and so on. All the requirements for ongoing development to keep up with market and oil company requirements. All seemed set for a good future. Not primarily in aviation, which was always my real, driving interest, but on the edge of the aircraft industry with the refuelling equipment, hydrant systems and associated equipment.

And then it happened. The unbelievable, again.

The Managing Director, Ron Mitchell, who had engaged me in the first place and who had given me so much support, was told to leave the company. The parent company, W.T. Avery, had decided that the profit margin of Avery Hardoll was too small, or even non-existent. Rightly or wrongly, in these situations, it is the man at the top, the Managing Director, who is held responsible and who has to go and be replaced. I do not know of course what exactly took place. I do know that he was deeply upset. He and his wife had just become settled in a house they purchased on near-by Hayling Island and now they had to move away. He did obtain another position in another group elsewhere, but he was sadly missed by all at Avery Hardoll. He was quickly replaced by a new managing director, who came down from the parent Avery group in Birmingham. He came with the reputation as a "hatchet man" to sort out and re-structure the company back into an acceptable profit.

Everything seemed to move along reasonably for a while and then changes began. One Friday, without any warning, I received a message from the MD's office – please come and see me immediately. I went and was informed that I was to lose my job as Technical Manager and become technical assistant to the Managing Director. I said that I was about to leave for a standards meeting in Europe, because I was on one of the Standards Committees setting up standards to fit in with the new European requirements. I was involved in several other activities of that sort in my role as Technical Manager. (There was no Technical Director. It was Avery policy that the subsidiary companies would only have two directors – Managing and Director/Secretary.) The response was that that activity fitted very well into the new proposed post of technical assistant to the MD. But I would have no department or staff and therefore no ongoing role in the development of new products. My place would be taken by someone that worked for me.

I was naturally disturbed and upset, especially at the wording and tone of the proposed notice that would be posted, which I was shown. I could see that in some ways this could be an opportunity, but the wording of the notice did not reflect that in any way. I asked if it could be modified and suggested some alternative wording. After some negotiation, wording was agreed. We shook hands and the MD took the gin bottle out of the boardroom cupboard and we had a drink on the new arrangement with the revised notice. It was by then evening and I went home to reflect on this quite dramatic change.

On Monday morning I returned to my office to find a note from the MD, come and see me. So I did, immediately. 'I've changed my mind,' he said. 'I'm not prepared to change the wording of the notice. It must stay as original.' I was staggered and said that I didn't understand and was not happy. I asked for time to think it over. 'All right,' he said, 'Go home for an hour if you wish, think it over and come back to me immediately.' So, I went home had a think, but decided that I could not accept such a change after our agreement. So I went back and reported accordingly. 'Right,' he said 'In that case your services are no longer required. Clear your desk and be out of here by 12 noon.'

End of story. End of my career with Avery. I was paid to the end of the year. But I decided that I'd had enough. I would never, ever again, work for anyone else.

I had some money until the end of the year and that gave me a little time to reflect and make decisions. What had I done wrong? I don't know, but no use looking back. Move forward and get on with something. Avery Hardoll had always been wedded to an aircraft refuelling coupling based on the idea of cam operation. This meant that the coupling had first to be engaged to the aircraft by a rotary movement, engaging lugs on the coupling with matching slots on the aircraft adaptor. Further rotary movement would then operate an internal cam that caused the coupling valve to open. The competition used a coupling that engaged to the aircraft in the same way, but the coupling valve was then opened by a lever. This meant two separate operations by the refuelling operator. This competitive coupling (developed and made in the USA) was popular with some operators, but had the disadvantage of being longer in length. I had for some time felt that there was an opening for a lever operated coupling of a design that would not infringe the American patent.

So, here was the opportunity. I quickly made myself a drawing board at home and started on a design. Then came the question of making a prototype and the associated cost. I received support and encouragement from many people, not the least of which were my cousins in America and a friend of theirs, originally from Norway. He was involved with the Norwegian resistance movement and emigrated to America shortly after the war. (He has, incidentally, recently co-written a book about his experiences – *Reckless Courage*). I had often stayed with my cousin Al on my trips to America and had, of course, met his Norwegian friend, Jack. They were enthusiastic about my project and invested funds to enable me to have a prototype made. At that point I registered a company and, of course, I had to have a name. In honour of my cousin Al and his friend Jack, I named my company Aljac Engineering Ltd. I am proud to be able to record that the name still exists to this day.

So started a whole new chapter in my life. I had a company of my own. I was not going to work for anyone else. I would be independent, make my own decisions and live with the consequences. The history of Aljac Engineering is a story in itself, but before embarking on that, it is perhaps, worth recording some of my experiences in flying on the many trips that I made over the years.

Chapter 13

Flying as a Passenger

My very first flight was while at Dowty Equipment Ltd., as described in Chapter 5. This was in 1948 and things were only just beginning to move again. Even that very first flight was not without incident, flying in fog and bad visibility was not fun. And later, as I will describe, I suffered a few incidents that were somewhat off-putting.

But let me say at the start that civilian flying is, in fact, a very safe form of travel compared to any other mode of transport. It is unfortunate that the very rare incidents attract the media and much publicity. Also, of course, if a large civil aircraft goes down there can, inevitably, be a large loss of life. But compared, for example, to the loss of life on our own roads amounting to several thousand every year, very small indeed.

I recount the incidents that I experienced simply because they were, shall we say, interesting, to an aircraft engineer, even if a little worrying for a while. But they do illustrate how a well maintained modern aircraft can tolerate the occasional malfunction and bad weather conditions. It all goes to demonstrate the comparative safety of air travel. I should perhaps add that when I first started to fly as a passenger I could not help listening to all the noises and working out what was going on. Operation of undercarriage, flaps and so on. Eventually I learnt to switch off and just relax, enjoy the sky and clouds. Even sleep occasionally!

Incident number one. I first flew the Atlantic sometime around 1952 – not sure exactly. The aircraft was the Boeing Stratocruiser, developed from a wartime Boeing bomber. It took something like thirteen hours London/New York, with a stop at Shannon to refuel. The actual crossing was overnight and, since I was on business and fortunate enough to travel first class, there was a bunk over the seat. One had to climb up a ladder to retire to the bunk and then draw a curtain. This was at the forward end of the aircraft and in line with the engines and propellers. Very noisy – not conducive to much sleep. At that time I was wearing a leg iron and climbing up to the bunk this became detached and tangled up on something. With other passengers watching, it was embarrassing! The aircraft itself was actually quite comfortable, with a lower deck bar and seating. The incident was on the return flight. One engine failed. The pilot feathered the propeller and just carried on as normal, while we sat looking at a stationary propeller. He came on the intercom and said nothing to worry about, we carry on as normal. I heard later that the Stratocruiser was known as the best three engined aircraft in the business.

Incident number two. I was in the USA visiting a company in Dayton, Ohio, who were licensees to Avery Hardoll, for whom I was working at the time. I received a message that our works manager was at that time also on a visit to Toronto, Canada and it would be a good time to meet up, since Dayton and Toronto were not all that far apart. It was winter time and the weather was not all that good, but it seemed a good idea, so I booked a flight from Ohio to Montreal and turned up at the airport at the appointed time. The weather deteriorated and all flights were cancelled. Not unusual in those days. They said it might be worth waiting for a while as it may clear up. I waited for what seemed like ages and then an announcement. There was a short gap in the weather and a flight would be leaving for Toronto shortly. I was anxious to get there so I took up the offer and boarded. The aircraft was a DC3 (a conversion from the wartime Dakota) and would normally take around thirty passengers. Take-off time arrived. I then realised I was the only passenger on the aircraft. Everybody else had declined.

We took off and shortly the weather deteriorated dramatically. Heavy gusts of wind with the aircraft all over the sky. The stewardess offered me, the only passenger, a cup of coffee which seemed like a good idea, but in practice was almost impossible. I managed a few sips before the rest finished up on the cabin ceiling. The stewardess said, 'Never mind, it will get cleared up later.' She then sat in a seat opposite and spent the rest of the flight saying prayers with a Rosary, carefully going through one bead at a time. We eventually landed at Toronto in a snowstorm and we were the last aircraft to land before they closed the airport. An interesting trip!

Incident number three. Again, while I was working for Avery Hardoll. This was probably the most difficult of all to contend with. I was on a visit to the USA, covering many visits to various companies and organisations with whom we were associated, one way or the other. I had to see someone in Los Angeles, California and I had another appointment arranged back on the East Side in upstate New York. After that it would be home. It was my habit to telephone the office on most days to see if there was anything needed, or anything that I should know about. So, before leaving Los Angeles, I duly telephoned. The Managing Director, Ron Mitchell, came on the line and told me that a problem had developed in Tokyo, something to do with hydrant pit valves. He asked me to go on to Tokyo and sort it out. But, I said, I have an appointment back in upstate New York that I must keep. (I think it was with Veeder Root, the manufacturer of petrol pump computers). OK, said the MD, keep that appointment and then go on to Tokyo and sort out their problem.

So, that's what I did. This meant flying from LA back to New York straight away. And then, instead of going home, getting a flight to Tokyo. For some reason this went back through Los Angeles, where another flight was taken to Tokyo which stopped briefly at Hawaii to refuel. My brief memory of Hawaii was very pleasant. Lots of sunshine and palm trees and girls in grass skirts performing a welcoming dance. And so on to Tokyo. We arrived over the airfield and, as what was not unusual in those days, went to the top of a stack of aircraft waiting for clearance to land. The procedure was to circle round at the allotted height level and then, when directed by flying control, to drop down a level. This continued until, eventually, we came in to land. Around on finals, lined up with the runway, then, engines throttled back, gradually descending to land. Not much to see – visibility was bad. Then suddenly, with no warning, engines opened up and rapid climb back up to the top of the stack. No word from the pilot or crew. No explanation, silence. All the passengers wondering what on earth was going on.

So, it started all over again. Circling gradually dropping down one level at a time. Only this time, looking out of the window, there was another aircraft that appeared to be at the same level circling 180 degrees away from us! Could there really have been two aircraft at the same level in the stack? This is certainly what it looked like. Still no word from the crew as to what was going on. Eventually, we came in to land, as before. Only this time we did actually land. Only then did the captain come on the intercom and say, 'Sorry about all that ladies and gentlemen, when we came in the first time there was another aircraft on the runway.' Another aircraft on the runway just where our 'plane was about to land! What happened to ground control? Was it tea-time or something?

We taxied to the terminal and disembarked and it was pouring with rain. Not only was it raining, but it was dull and overcast, with heavy, dark clouds, full of foreboding. As soon as I had cleared customs and the usual formalities I was met by our agents. They wanted to take me immediately on to the airfield to investigate the reported faulty refuelling hydrant pit.

Now, it was around 5pm Tokyo time. I had been flying for a long time – probably over 16 hours or more? Things took longer in those days. I was totally adrift on time and I had crossed the date line. I had no idea what day it was, or what time my body said it was. I was half asleep, had just been through a slightly stressful time in the air. And it was pouring with rain. And I was to go out on the airfield, look intelligent and come up with a diagnosis of a reported problem immediately! No thank you... I explained to the agent and, to be fair, they understood – at least I think they did. In any event, I had a rest, some refreshment and then ventured out.

This is not the place to discuss the problem, even if I could remember what it was, but I can record that whatever it was it was solved to everyone's satisfaction.

I was asked to stay for a while in Tokyo and make a few more visits, but by then I had really had enough. I stayed for a couple of days to be polite and then went home.

Incident number four. There was one other minor incident. Later, on another trip to the USA, we were flying in to New York. I sensed something was not quite right. The aircraft was flying slowly in a circle and I could hear, I thought, a noise of hydraulics that I couldn't understand. There was nothing wrong with the weather this time, clear sky and fine. The aircraft was circling around. What was the delay?

Eventually the captain came on the intercom – 'Good afternoon, ladies and gentlemen, we will shortly be landing at JFK, New York and we will not be landing in the usual area. We will be using a special landing strip across the other side of the airport. When you look out of the window, you will see that there are fire engines and ambulances grouped around our landing area. Please do not worry about this. There is nothing to be concerned about, although this is unusual. What has happened is that we have experienced a total loss of hydraulic power and we have had to lower the landing gear and will operate the flaps by using the emergency hand pump, which, of course, will take longer. The airport authorities decided that we should land in the emergency landing area, just as a precaution. Similarly, the emergency vehicles are there simply as a precaution. This is standard procedure in this kind of situation.'

Nothing to worry about, he said. And I could believe that. I'm not sure if all the passengers thought the same way. Anyway, we landed completely normally, no problem. We taxied over to the terminal (or perhaps we were towed, it was, of course a longer distance than usual) and disembarked normally. Nothing more was said.

It is important to point out that I only quote these instances to show that, yes, sometimes things don't quite go to plan, but the skill that went into the design, manufacture and testing of the aircraft, together with the skill and training of the flight crew ensures that, except in some very rare examples, the aircraft and passengers suffer no more than perhaps a late arrival at their destination. And perhaps a few anxious moments in the meanwhile!

Flying as a passenger is a very safe means of travel compared to other transport methods.

Chapter 14

Aljac Engineering Ltd

With my home made drawing board, I continued with my design of an alternative refuelling coupling. What I wanted to achieve was the more popular lever operated coupling, but with the more compact size of the Avery Hardoll cam operated design. Many sheets of paper and a few pencils later I came up with what, to me, looked like something worth trying. So, on to some detail drawings. I finally had in my hand a full set of detail drawings ready for manufacture. But what now? I needed to get a prototype made and tested. The next step would be to demonstrate it to the major oil companies. As mentioned earlier, my American cousin and his friend Jack wanted to support me and I will be eternally grateful to them for their encouragement and financial support that enabled me to have a prototype made. The way I was able to do that is a story in itself. Some near neighbours at the time were running a business in restoring aircraft engines. Their main customer at that time was the Israel Army. They were using tanks fitted with ex-aircraft engines which needed much restoration and the engines were shipped over to the UK, restored, converted to military armoured vehicle use and shipped back. At the time, a nice little business. Unfortunately, two things happened that changed everything. The owner of the business sadly passed away and his widow was struggling to keep things going. At the same time, the Israel business began to dry up and work was hard to find.

I was able to come to an arrangement whereby my prototype and, hopefully, follow-on work for Aljac Engineering, would be made in the company's workshops. On a proper commercial basis of course. In return, I undertook to assist in managing the company. I had my salary from Avery Hardoll until the end of the year, so did not need anything else from the business. Hopefully, by the end of the year, Aljac would be able to support me from incoming orders.

My prototype coupling was made and tested as far as I was able. It seemed to work well and showed promise. I believed that since it was to compete with the American version, it would be best to demonstrate it to the US oil companies first. So, I made arrangements to take it to the USA. Meanwhile, I was receiving much support and encouragement from the UK oil company executives that I had come to know as a result of my work at Avery Hardoll. I was invited by Shell International to tender for a quantity of four water-methanol dispensers. At that time, certain turbo-prop engine aircraft needed an injection of cooling water for some periods of engine operation. A turbo-prop engine is basically a jet engine, but the flow of hot gases after combustion is used to drive a turbine coupled to a conventional propeller, whereas in a pure jet engine, the flow of hot gases is exhausted through the tail pipe, resulting in a thrust that drives the aircraft forward. In the turbo-prop version, the very hot gases of combustion would be directed to the turbine driving the propeller. Consequently, the turbine blades needed cooling, hence the need for cooling water carried on the aircraft. Methanol was added as a non-corrosive protection against freezing. It seemed entirely logical that the oil company supplying the turbine fuel should be able to replenish the water-methanol at the same time. Hence the reason for Shell going out to tender for dispensers. Anyway, I quickly produced sufficient drawings for estimating purposes, taking care, of course, that they would meet the specification.

I cannot recall the exact sequence of events, but around that time, my refuelling coupling was ready for demonstration and I arranged a trip to the USA to show my coupling to the US oil company aviation departments. (see photograph in plates)

Again, I am pleased to record that I received much encouragement. I think the manner of my dismissal from Avery Hardoll had gone the rounds and several of the executives I met seemed determined to help in any way they could. At the same time, of course, any equipment I produced had to be right and would only be chosen after the usual rigorous testing and approval. It should be pointed out that any product or equipment taken up and used by an oil company has to meet rigorous standards and conform to their quality standards. This is particularly so with anything remotely to do with aviation and flying. An item such as a refuelling coupling has to conform to the oil company standard, be tested thoroughly and, eventually, approved. It then appears on the oil company approved list and their buyers are authorised to invite tenders from that manufacturer. This may seem somewhat complicated just to put fuel into the aircraft, but, in fact, fuel quality and accuracy of delivery to the aircraft are a fundamental and critical part of aircraft safety. The good part of this sometimes lengthy and detailed procedure, is that once a piece of equipment is approved the oil company takes full responsibility. Without exception, I have always found the oil company executives with whom I have dealt over the years to be strictly honourable and always willing to help.

So, I took my coupling to the USA on a scheduled passenger flight, carrying it as a piece of hand luggage. I had a few problems explaining it at Heathrow, but nothing compared to the reception at New York Customs and Immigration Control. I had much explaining to do. But everybody was helpful and trying to understand. I had to try and explain what it was and how it worked. And, more important, why was I, an ordinary passenger, carrying such a thing? One thing I learnt was not to try to be funny with US customs. It just doesn't work. But eventually I was allowed through. I cannot imagine what would happen these days, I am sure it would not be allowed. I went on and was probably met by my cousin Al. They lived on Long Island and I stayed with them. I will be eternally grateful for their support. I made some appointments with oil company personnel and it is perhaps worth recording my first exposure to what was then the American way of doing things.

I have often recalled how I went in to New York City with a pocket full of dimes (the cost of a local telephone call at that time), and called up the aviation executive of an oil company from a local 'phone box to make an appointment. Without exception, I was well received and offered appointments – sometimes immediately. 'Come on over, pleased to see you,' was quite normal it seemed.

I couldn't help contrasting with the attitude of a UK oil company executive (who shall be nameless) with whom I wanted an appointment. He said he was very busy – didn't really have time, but if I really wanted some of his precious time it would have to be at 8.00am before he became involved in anything else (more important than me I presumed). I said OK and asked for a day. This was agreed. I don't know how I did it from south Hampshire, but on the appointed day, I arrived at the London office concerned, well before the appointed time, only to be told that something else had cropped up and he did not have the time to see me! What a contrast to the US! Even allowing for the fact that I had arrived in New York unexpectedly, my reception was completely different and very refreshing. It is a two way thing, because it encourages good feeling and a willingness to do everything possible to help. At the same time, it is, of course, commercial. The oil company wants a piece of equipment that meets with their approval, will do something for them and, above all, is a commercial proposition and competitive. From the equipment supplier's standpoint, it has to be profitable, so that a fledgling company like Aljac can survive and, eventually, prosper.

So, I was able to make a quick appointment with a US oil company executive responsible for aircraft refuelling. I duly turned up at the appointed hour complete with my coupling to demonstrate. Again, I had some security problems in getting past the front desk, but a quick telephone call soon put that right. I presented myself, complete with coupling, which I proudly displayed. The executive was very patient and spent some time looking at it, handling it and checking its weight. Then he said something that to this day I haven't fully understood what was intended. He said, thoughtfully, 'In America, we have an expression, – if it looks right, it probably is.' I truly don't know whether that meant that it looked good to him, or whether he thought there was still some work to do. In any event, the end result looked good, because it was agreed that the coupling would be placed on trial at an upstate airfield and this was arranged.

I continued on my visit, saw a number of other people and then went home, knowing that my coupling was to be tried. Later I had a message that it was in use and appeared to be working fine. And then came the bad news. All seemed to be going well until, after one refuelling operation, the coupling jammed on the aircraft and the operator could not remove it. It had to be dismantled in order to get it off the aircraft tank adapter. This must have meant some delay to the scheduled service, which is always bad news and incurs costs. But, as always, the oil company were very good about it and accepted the responsibility. Another reason why it was so good to deal with them, even though sometimes it could be difficult. As far as my coupling was concerned, it was not difficult to see and put right the problem that had caused it to jam on the aircraft. I altered the design drawings, but there it was left because other things intervened and it was a question of priorities. Then the whole world changed. I received the order from Shell International for the four water-methanol dispensers for which I had quoted.

Detailed manufacturing drawings were quickly produced and serious work commenced. The very first order! The tanks were sub-contracted out, but much of the work was able to be done within the company that I had the arrangement with. We eventually produced the four dispensers and received some publicity.

There had been some concern when the Shell inspector came down to check and sign them off. He was not happy with a particular construction method we had chosen for the pressurised tanks, but agreed to accept them and duly signed the paperwork. I was very happy indeed to deliver the goods and raise an invoice for our very first order. Another great advantage of working for an oil company then became apparent. Invoices were paid in thirty days, no quibble. To a fledgling company, struggling to progress with very little finance, cash flow is all important. To be kept waiting for payment when suppliers invoices have to be met, workers paid and materials purchased for future orders, can spell disaster, which is why many small and embryo companies fail. So, I received payment and also further enquiries. Things were starting to happen. I was able to engage a draughtsman and one or two others to help. And, course, I was still helping to manage the engine re-conditioning business. Then another change in direction, which would probably have happened anyway.

There was some family intervention in the engine re-conditioning business. It was to change direction. This is not the place to go into details, but the upshot was that I was asked to leave and take my business elsewhere. I had been thinking, in any case, that it was time to move on. We looked like securing some more orders and I had designs in my head for new products that I wanted to get on with. So, after looking around, I found a small factory unit in the area that was available on a six month lease and at an affordable rent. It was small, but it would serve the purpose and enable me to start on developing the company into something serious. I decided that if I was not able to have a going concern within six months, then it was hardly worth proceeding. On the other hand, I had definitely decided that I would never work for anyone else again – so it had to be successful. Another big factor in starting any business is finance. Without private finance, the only way forward is to secure an overdraft from the bank. I went to the local branch of the bank that my family had used for many years and pleaded my case.

I was offered almost anything I wanted as long as I was prepared to use my house as security. This I refused to do. I said that I was prepared to work all the hours of the day and sometimes half the night as well, but what I would not do, under any circumstances, was to jeopardise the security of my family, with dependent children. In these circumstances, the bank would only offer me a limited overdraft and that had to suffice. Therefore I developed my small business accordingly.

But things did progress and we secured a few more orders that kept things going. I began to think about strainers and filters as a market that could be exploited and felt that I could improve the design of fluid strainers on the market. I worked on this aspect and eventually produced a design that could be fabricated and would not require a large investment in tooling. At the same time I began to be interested in a small industrial development taking place in the local town of Petersfield. Relatively small factory units were to be built and one of them looked as though it would be ideal for my purpose. Furthermore, it would be ready at just about the time that the present six-month tenure would run out. Once again, destiny was playing into my hands and in due course we moved into the new factory unit that was to be a happy home for the next few years. I was able to engage workers and some staff and equip the workshop with machinery, welding and fabrication equipment and, in fact everything necessary to produce the products that I was designing including the new design of fabricated strainer for which orders were being received.

I was able to develop a small drawing office and to begin a serious sales effort. The range of fabricated strainers were selling quite well, but I needed to be working on something closer to my real love – aviation, so I sought enquiries in that area. A number of opportunities developed.

We were invited by an oil company to tender for a complete aircraft refuelling station in Libya. By this time I was ready to engage a draughtsman and we were able to prepare a reasonable set of drawings for quotation purposes. We obtained the order and successfully built and tested satisfactorily the complete unit, which was shipped out to Libya. This order confirmed our ability to undertake such work, needing a design capability, very tight quality control and a commensurate manufacturing capability.

By this time, things were going reasonably well and orders were coming in. In particular, we received orders for a number of mobile, trailer driven refuelling units, which were very well received. Anything remotely connected with aviation demanded my enthusiasm. (see photograph)

I had engaged a draughtsman/designer, a works manager, a secretary and a workforce of about fourteen, with a foreman. We needed a proper inspection arrangement and I was able to engage an inspector. Christmas came and I was so pleased with everybody that I organised a Christmas dinner with everything paid for. It was, of course, well received, but the drink flowed far too freely at the free bar and I finished up with an incapable workforce for the rest of the day! The following year I changed the arrangements. The meal was free, but all drinks had to be paid for. What a difference!

Then the first near disaster. The three-day week at the time of the miner's strike. Neither the government of the day, or the miners union, were going to give in. The result of that was, apart from other inconveniences, the electricity generating stations that depended on coal for their fuel were running out. Electricity supply was running out. Neither side was prepared to give in, so the government decreed that industry would have to reduce to a three day week. My solution that I put to the workers was that if they would work twelve hours a day for three days, I would still pay them for a normal 40 hour week. This was agreed. I kept the office open and we operated without electricity. When it got too dark to work, we used candles and an oil lamp, which I still have displayed to this day. In spite of the problems, we survived in one piece and eventually the miner's dispute was settled.

The second drama was completely unexpected and I would think is almost unique in industry. One day, going around the works as was my custom, I came across a drawing that I did not recognise. I asked about it. 'What is this?' I asked of several people around. Noone seemed to know until it became obvious that I was not going to let it rest. Someone mumbled something about it being a "foreigner", workshop slang for somebody's private work being done on the side, a practice not unknown in larger companies and often ignored in the interests of good relations. But further examination of the rather grubby and tattered drawing in question showed a name that appeared to be that of another company, rather than a private individual. I confiscated the drawing of course and traced the name to a local organisation. I telephoned them and was told, 'Oh, yes, that's a part being made for us by a sub-contractor in Petersfield. They often do work for us.'

Finally, the penny dropped and it began to dawn on me that I had been too trusting and that things were going on that I knew nothing about. I realised that this was on a scale that was beyond the scope of the odd "foreigner" being made on the sly during factory hours. So I decided to mount a watch. One evening I went back to the industrial estate and hid myself round the corner, where I could see the Aljac factory, but remain hidden. I was determined to stay there until something happened. All night if necessary. And then it did happen. Two figures appeared, went to the factory side door, produced a key and opened. Shortly afterwards lights appeared and machinery was running. I went to the door that they had left unlocked, and entered.

144

I could hardly believe what I found. My trusted foreman and the design/draughtsman working away in my factory, producing someone else's product. My immediate response was, 'Get out – now! And both come and see me in the office in the morning.' And then I demanded the duplicate key which they gave me without argument. They left and after a quick look round, I left for what was left of the night to calm down and think it over. But there was no question as to what had to be done. They had to go. In the morning they duly presented themselves in my office and tried to explain. They thought they were doing no harm and were earning something on the side. Tax free of course. I felt particularly sorry for my foreman. He had come from New Zealand and had experienced a difficult time until I took him on. I felt sure that he had been misled by the designer draughtsman. But they both held senior positions in our fledgling company and had betrayed my trust. There was only one answer. 'You are both dismissed with immediate effect. Salary due will be sent to you… Go, now.' They went and I heard no more. It left a gap, but we struggled on and made arrangements to cope. Orders were still coming in. And then, another drama.

The third drama was again totally unexpected. With increasing business for the very quality conscious oil companies, it was necessary to have a good inspection department with a qualified inspector. I advertised and a number of people applied. I engaged someone who had been an inspector in a recognised company and seemed to be ideal, friendly and someone I could work with. Why don't I ever learn? One day the new inspector came to my office and announced, 'All your men have joined the Union and I have been appointed their shop steward. In future you will deal with me on all matters affecting the shop floor.' From then on, his whole attitude changed. I had come to learn something about him and his family situation. (I always tried to take an interest in the welfare of those that worked for me.) I had learnt that he lived on his own with a daughter who was not at all well. I went round to see her and, I think, took a small gift. It seemed to be appreciated at the time, but now everything changed and he became remote and very official.

At that time I continued my normal interest in the welfare of those that worked for me, but it did not seem to make any difference. I recall one instance that perhaps is a lesson. One of the workers did not turn up and I asked around if he had a problem. Did anyone know anything? Nothing specific emerged, but I got the impression that something was amiss. So, one evening I called round to his house, on a local council estate. The house was in darkness, but I knocked and, eventually the door was very carefully opened just a crack, enough to see who I was. I was admitted; to find the family huddled round just one bar of an electric fire and in total darkness, except for a candle. It was very cold in the room and they were wearing winter outer clothing. They were sharing a packet of fish and chips, straight from a newspaper wrapping. It appeared that was all the family had to eat. I wanted to know what was going on, he was earning quite good money.

Eventually, it all came out. A loan shark was operating in the area. He had knocked on the door and offered to lend them an amount of money unheard of that would enable them, as a family, to have and enjoy unheard of luxuries. And, of course, it was followed by grossly extortionate interest rates that they couldn't possibly afford. And then the inevitable follow-up of thugs knocking on the door and demanding payment. So, they had to sell most things, most of their furniture and anything else that was saleable to pay off the debt. My worker was in a state of shock and was totally confused. I helped to get them sorted out and he came back to work. But how many others fall prey to taking up a loan with extortionate interest rates that they cannot afford to pay, even to this day?

At that time we were very busy in the workshop and overtime was being worked. I always tried to be careful to offer overtime on as even a distribution basis as possible, consistent with the nature of the workload and the skills of the people concerned. Inevitably, it depended to some extent on the nature of incoming orders and promised delivery dates. Obviously, the men were glad to earn the extra money, but at the same time they had the flexibility to choose when to work overtime, within reason. I thought the arrangement was satisfactory for all concerned and there were certainly no complaints. Until one day the newly appointed shop steward asked to see me and came to my office. He said that it was a question of the overtime being worked and announced, without any more pre-amble, 'We have decided that either everybody works overtime, or nobody works overtime,' I was dumbfounded at this approach when everything seemed to be going well and tried to open a discussion, but to no avail. He was adamant, there was nothing to discuss, the position was simple. Everybody works or nobody works overtime. There was only one answer to that. 'Then nobody works. End of overtime.' He went back to the shop floor. I don't know what he told the men, but the position stayed the same. They would not work overtime and I would not give in.

We began to suffer on production of orders and, worse than that, the men started to leave and take jobs elsewhere where they could work all hours and earn the extra money they needed. I learned afterwards that there was more to it than that, but more of that later. This went on and things were getting really desperate, until there were only a few men left. I had nothing more to lose. I called the shop steward into my office. I said, 'Your actions have meant that there are only a few men left. Your services are no longer required. Leave these premises immediately. Wages due plus an extra week will be forwarded.'

He expostulated, 'You can't do that!'

'I just did,' I said. 'Go, now.' He went. Naturally, he took me to the Industrial Tribunal and pleaded unfair dismissal. I attended personally and simply explained what had happened. My explanation was accepted and the tribunal dismissed the case but awarded the complainant an extra two weeks wages.

After all this, the men gradually came back to work as before. Eventually, every single one returned to their original jobs and overtime continued as before. I was curious and I asked them – why? What happened? Then they told me. They had been told by my trusted inspector that they must all join the Union. If they did not, he would see to it that they would never, ever, get another job in the Portsmouth area. So they conformed. The result was nearly the end of a fledgling company, another enterprise lost.

There was a sequel to all this. A few weeks afterwards I received a telephone call from a very large Portsmouth company, part of a large national group. Would I please give a reference for an inspector who had just applied for a job? I said yes, he was a good inspector, but went on to say be careful about relations. I was interrupted quite rudely – 'Thank you, but we will take care of that. We only want from you a reference to the man's inspection capability.' So that was that. Except that, not more than about a month later there was a headline in the local paper along the lines – 'Local company on strike. Hundreds of workers affected.' But the photograph! It was a photograph of a group of workers and the man in middle of the group, the man who had organised the strike, no less than my ex-inspector!

But back in my small company, things were slowly moving ahead. We were beginning to get back into the aviation side that was always my consuming interest. Enquiries were coming in for aircraft refuelling hydrant dispensers and similar equipment. At the same time, I had met on my visit to the USA, a company Gammon Technical Products (GTP) and their founder Howard Gammon. I had probably been introduced by one of the US oil companies, who held Howard and his company in high regard in the field of aviation fuel quality control. I seemed to get on very well with them

147

and I was offered a license to manufacture and distribute their products in the UK. I was delighted to take this up and it opened a whole new area of business. We manufactured the Gammon Differential Pressure gauge, used to measure the pressure differential across filter/water separators in the aircraft re-fuelling process. An absolutely fundamental aid to quality control and therefore safety.

The differential pressure across the filter elements is a measure of the degree of contamination and at the specified level the filter elements would be renewed. This was right up my street, at the heart of aviation safety and reliability. It would eventually be manufactured by Aljac in considerable numbers. Something like thirty per month were made and sold for a long time.

Things were looking up. And then the next drama began to unfold. We had quoted Iran (at that time Persia) for a large quantity of our fabricated strainer and the order came – something like £130,000 worth, which at that time, 1975, was a considerable sum. (see photograph in plates)

The order came through an agent there and I telephoned him to discuss how payment would be made. It was normal for export orders to ask for a Letter of Credit, held by the bank and payable when proof of export was shown. The agent told me that this procedure was not acceptable to their authorities. It had to be on trust, with an invoice payable through the bank on receipt of the goods. I was assured that this was normal and that the Iranian customer was totally reliable and trustworthy. After some thought I accepted and we proceeded with the order. (see photograph in plates)

Recently, I happened to be in the area and went to have a look at the industrial estate. The factory unit that was Aljac is still there. It seems very small now to have undertaken such a large order.

It was hard going for our small fabrication section, but it was essential that delivery dates were met. Each and every strainer had to be pressure tested. I recall testing the last batch myself, working through the night when everybody else had gone. Delivery was made and the correct paperwork raised. Then disaster. The customer had raised the correct paperwork for the bank to release payment against our invoice, but there was an error. Careful examination showed that this was merely a typing error, the paperwork had to match exactly, in every detail, or the bank would not release the money. I protested, but to no avail, it would have to go back and be corrected at source before money could be released. This placed me in an impossible position. I had to pay for materials and labour. And other orders were coming in for which finance was required to manufacture.

There was only one option. Go to my bank manager and ask for a temporary increase in our overdraft. The manager listened, but said that yes, they could do that, but only with increased security. I would have to use the house as security. I said no. In no circumstances would I risk the house. In that case, said the manager, we can't help you. I protested and asked for it to be referred to a higher level, but the answer was the same. No house, no increase in the overdraft, not even on a temporary basis. So I went away to have a long, hard think. I decided that I was not going to give in and that I would have to look for finance elsewhere. I had a few contacts and searched around, eventually making contact with someone who thought they could help. I was introduced to the Crystalate Group of companies, who were strong in plastics, telephone communications equipment and associated electronics. Apparently they had been thinking of adding engineering to their portfolio and Aljac, although relatively small, seemed to fit. I was asked to their London head office to meet with the directors. This seemed to go well and it resulted in an offer being made to purchase Aljac shares and help to finance the company. In return, I would remain as Managing Director and would be appointed to the Crystalate board as a Group Director. This seemed a good opportunity, not only to keep Aljac going, but to open up a whole new field of experience for me as a Group Director of a major industrial group of companies. I accepted and a whole new set of experiences began.

The problem with the strainer order paperwork was quickly sorted out and the money received. It is worth recording that the Iranian authorities at that time did, in fact, act honourably. The problem was purely in the paperwork and the very strict procedures of the bank concerned, who could not, or would not, accept an obvious typing error.

Around that time, we began to run out of space. We were attracting many more enquiries for various forms of aircraft and helicopter refuelling dispensers, both static and mobile. This was the side of the business that was obviously close to my heart and kept me in touch with my first love, aviation in all its forms. We moved to much larger premises in Emsworth, the old steam laundry in fact. This gave room for a much enlarged machine shop and fabrication facility, a larger office space with proper secretarial facilities and a small, but vital, drawing office. Most important, it was possible to create a larger, fit for purpose, outside test facility, capable of testing the larger equipment we were attracting enquiries for, including complete refuelling tankers, previously beyond our scope. Parts of the building that we did not use were sub-let, which helped with the all important cash flow. One tenant was creating a new business importing from the USA what was then the latest gadget – mobile 'phones. Enormous and cumbersome by present day standards, but the start of a prosperous business.

The prospects looked good and I was beginning to enjoy my new role. I attended group board meetings in London, but not sure I could make much contribution at that stage, except to report on progress at Aljac. The group chairman had a villa in the south of France, at Valbonne, and occasionally called for a board meeting down there. Some of the directors came with their wives and stayed in the villa, which was on three or four floors. I stayed in the local small hotel. We did have board meetings, but I did not perform very well suffering from the usual stomach problem with too much strange food. There were two experiences worth recording. We had to play the mandatory game of golf at the local golf club. It was my first exposure to how much goes on and how many decisions are reached in apparent casual conversation on the golf course. A number of things were said to me of which I did not understand the full significance at the time. I had not been playing golf for very long and was not doing very well. Someone said to me at one time, 'You obviously know very well how to play golf, but…' It was some time before I realised that my colleagues took all of this as part of the overall scene of being a group director and just played along with the chairman and enjoyed the break.

Then the matter of the geraniums. The chairman's villa had an outside terrace right at the very top and the chairman was in the habit of calling meetings there, and certainly it was very pleasant in the warm climate of southern France. The terrace had flower borders around the edges, in stone work and about 3 feet high. Chairs were set around in a rough circle for our meeting. And then the chairman would produce his favourite liquor to help us along. This was a substance pronounced locally "mark", not sure how it was spelt in French. For me, it tasted horrible and was beyond me to drink. It was not on to refuse the chairman's proffered drink, so what to do? It so happened that I was quite close to one of the borders, with geraniums in full bloom. Being careful that the chairman was looking the other way, I poured my drink into the geraniums. Nobody noticed. But the following year, at another gathering at Valbonne, the chairman announced a mystery that he could not understand. A section of the geraniums had turned white! I knew that it was the section immediately behind where I had been sitting the previous year, but nobody else seemed to connect.

Meanwhile, back at the factory, things were developing. We received orders for small, complete, refuelling vehicles, notably for British Airways. (see photograph in plates)

But I was finding it very difficult to show a working profit. As part of the group, I was required to employ a Finance Manager and a Sales Manager, all of which attracted additional overheads. The theory was that the Sales Manager would attract the extra business to pay for the increased overheads, but extra business takes time to bring to fruition and in the meanwhile it was increasingly difficult to show a profit. It was a very worrying time and to add to my worries a relations problem developed in the workshop that was completely unexpected. I had always had good relations with those that worked for me, right back to the Gloster TDD days and I was very surprised. It concerned the foreman, who had always been helpful, co-operative and in general an excellent member of the team. But he seemed to be constantly trying to cause trouble concerning relations with him personally and with the workshop in general. I was completely mystified, but sensed that there was something not right. In the end, I called him into my office and confronted him.

'Now come on,' I said, 'It's obvious there's something wrong. What's going on?' There was some blustering and some vague suggestions but nothing specific. I was even more sure that I was not getting the true picture. 'There's more to this, isn't there? I know you too well. Come out with it, then we can deal with it.' He then broke down.

'Mr A,' he said through his tears, 'you don't understand. There are people out there, out to get you. They've been in here, in your office, they've been right through your filing cabinet, searched all your papers.' And so it went on and eventually the whole story came out. He was in some financial trouble and had been looking for help. He came across these people, probably in the local pub. I don't know, but whoever they were they offered him a deal. The deal was that he was to make a case against me that could be taken to the tribunal. They would help and provide information conjured up from what they had found.

The deal was that he would get compensation and the people would take a percentage. The whole thing collapsed and I heard no more. We obviously tightened our security. How often did it happen to others I wonder?

To return to the problem of running a business and showing a profit. This was getting more and more difficult. To cope with the imposed overheads and yet remain competitive to secure orders was a problem, although by this time we were becoming well known in the business and were still receiving many enquiries. As a Group Board Director, I naturally attended the regular group board meetings in London and made whatever contribution I could. I was asked to visit the other group companies from time to time and make any observations that were appropriate. I also attended some other group activities, which gave me good experience. I met some well known people that otherwise would have just been names to me. At the board meetings I reported on the progress of my own company, including the balance sheet. Not a lot was said. I tried to reassure the board that everything possible was being done, at the same time trying to deal with the overheads that were making progress difficult. Sympathetic noises were made by some of the other board members, but that was all. But nothing prepared me for what was to follow.

As a public group there was the annual AGM with the shareholders and the group board. It was in my third year in the group and I came prepared with my usual brief statement about Aljac, should it become necessary. Just before the start, the board members, as usual, gathered in an ante room for a brief discussion with the chairman on any matter that might arise. This was just before the meeting opened. The chairman came up to me and said – 'I'm going to have to report another loss from your company. That is unacceptable. You must resign.' I was dumbfounded.

'When?' I asked. 'Now,' he said, 'immediately, before the meeting.' I was in state of shock and disbelief, but I had no option. I went home.

As a side issue perhaps, but worth recording, at that time we were having a large order produced in another group company for a number of helicopter refuelling systems that we had designed. They were for a major oil company and destined for North Sea oil rigs. When they were finished and despatched, a works executive from the group company concerned said, 'Actually, they were quite profitable.' Ironic, but it made no difference.

Then the detail followed. My company had to leave the group, of course and that meant going back to the original agreement. When Aljac was taken into the Crystalate Group, they automatically, under the terms of the agreement, acquired all the assets of the company. Designs, patent rights, the lot. The agreement specified that the group would acquire all the assets for the nominal sum of one pound (which I never received). It also specified that if Aljac left the group, for any reason, the assets could be purchased back by Aljac at the current valuation. The assets included everything, machines, office furniture, work-in-progress, in fact every single thing that we had spent so long building up. But I did not have that sort of money and I was still not prepared to use the house as security, which would have been grossly unfair on my family. I was facing ruin and the loss of the business so dear to my heart. I would have to look for a job – and work for somebody else again? What happens? What do I do wrong? Why do I trust? And then came salvation.

One of the group directors, Charles Howe, came to my rescue and to him I am eternally grateful. He intervened on my behalf and negotiated a deal whereby I could have the assets back now and pay for them in a year's time. This was agreed. I returned to Emsworth and gave a great deal of thought as to what I should do. I wanted to continue in business, maintain my excellent relations with the oil companies so carefully built up over the years, but I had to make sufficient profit to pay off the debt to Crystalate within a year.

I eventually decided on the way ahead. First, the factory must close. I would have all manufacturing sub-contracted at a fixed price, so that I knew exactly what the selling price had to be. Then we had to move to smaller office premises and reduce the overheads. I would keep some staff – secretarial, book-keeping and design/draughtsman. I would do as much as possible myself, which meant working even longer hours. We would have to give up quoting for the larger refuelling tankers, because we would not have the facilities for testing. But we would keep all the other Aljac products going, including the small, mobile fuelling dispensers. We needed a sub-contractor that could carry out this type of testing and that had a good inspection and quality control capability. Fortunately, I found one that proved to be superb – Hilsea Engineering in Portsmouth. Totally reliable and trustworthy and pleased to have our kind of work. (see photograph)

I was very fortunate to have some wonderful people working for me. We were a great team. Some came and moved on, but, in particular, I remember Carol Sellen who worked hard on almost everything in the office and Peter Churchill who had worked for us at the old Emsworth laundry site and came back to handle all the design and draughting work, sadly, no longer with us. And, of course, my own daughter Juliet who handled incoming sales and the associated paperwork. As I say, a great team. No-one could wish for more.

We worked very hard for that year, but the end result was that the debt to Crystalate was paid in full, on time. I was now free and could get on with my business. I received enormous support and encouragement from the oil company staff that knew me, both here and in the USA. But, there was absolutely no favouritism. We had to be strictly competitive and produce the right goods on time, every time.

And so we went on. The business became stable. We were making a reasonable profit. Nothing dramatic, but enough to keep us going comfortably. I had developed many contacts. One in particular was with Sri Lanka, through an excellent agent that I will call Herbert. We developed some sales to the oil companies there and also did some work for the Sri Lanka Air Force, much of which came to nothing.

Security was a constant problem with the Tamil situation. I recall going to meetings at Air Force headquarters in Colombo with Herbert. We had to park the car at a different place each time. I didn't understand why at first, until Herbert explained, 'They will be watching who comes and goes.' They being the Tamils. When we left the car and walked to the Air Force entrance there was another surprise in store. There was a chicane formed by piled up sandbags, through which we had to walk. When we came out at the end, we found ourselves looking straight down the barrel of a 25 pounder gun, trained on the entrance, and I am quite sure ready to open fire if need be.

I produced a number of concepts for the Air Force, the most interesting being an air-transportable refueller designed for up-country operations, against the Tamils of course. It really looked as though an order was coming and I did some detail design and obtained quotations. One of the interesting experiences was being invited to Air Force headquarters to take part in a round table conference in which I was to present the air-transportable fueller, which would then be discussed. The Air Commodore, head of the air force, chaired the meeting and I made my presentation. But to no avail, no order was forthcoming. There were a number of other strange experiences in Sri Lanka, culminating in one that very nearly cost me my life.

At one time I was asked to organise a meeting with some officers to explain some of the concepts being talked about for development within the Air Force. The meeting was to be held in the hotel where I was staying in Colombo and it was supposed to be under very strict secrecy. It was emphasised to me that nobody was to be aware of what was taking place, so I duly arranged for a conference room and awaited the appointed time. Imagine my astonishment when the Air Force officers turned up, all at the same time and in uniform! So much for secrecy.

I was invited to give a talk on jet fuel quality control at one of the Air Force bases and was taken there by the Rear Commodore in his car, which had the windows completely blacked out for security. We drove up to the base and had to stop several hundred yards from the gate while the sentries identified the occupants through binoculars. Fine, but after the meeting I was driven back and on the way was invited to the Rear Commodore's house for a cup of tea. With the car, complete with blacked out windows parked outside the house!

As a matter of interest, I gave my talk, emphasising how important it was to adhere to laid down procedures in refuelling for quality control and personal safety, only to witness shortly afterwards a continuation of the procedure, in complete contrast to what I had been saying that was not only poor on quality control, but was also unsafe, placing the operator in personal danger. But I wonder who was right? They were getting the job done.

And so things continued and we were more or less stable. There were one or two interesting highlights. I needed another draughtsman and advertised. I received an application that looked promising and called the applicant for interview.

He seemed ideal, had all the right experience and I offered him the job. 'There's only one thing,' he said, 'I need four weeks off in the summer for an arrangement already booked.' I wanted to know why? He told me that he belonged to a charity, doing work in a poor region of India. They wanted to introduce modern methods of obtaining and purifying water and several other innovative ideas that would help the local villagers to live a better life and develop, for example, better hygiene. But the clever part and the reason he needed time off, was that instead of barging into the natives' village and trying to tell them what to do, they set up their own village nearby, presumably with the approval of the authorities and developed within their own village the techniques they wished to introduce. Obtaining and purifying water, generating some electricity by harnessing power from a local flowing stream and so on. The locals could not contain their curiosity and slowly began to come over, witness what was going on and copy for their own use in their own village. It worked. And the reason my applicant wanted the time off was because the charity members took it in turns to spend time in the village. I was impressed and he got the job.

As things progressed we were receiving more and more sales enquiries and I needed someone to handle the constant flow of paperwork. My youngest daughter had recently left school. I offered her the job, which she accepted and was very good. Many years later, long after retirement, she was on a visit. There was some inference in social conversation about my untidiness, fully justified these days I'm afraid. I was expostulating, 'I didn't used to be like this you know. In my business I always tidied up my desk. Everything went away at night time before going home.'

'That's not the way I remember it Dad,' came from daughter. Enough said!

The years went by and finally the time came to think about the future. I was now sixty-five, everything was going well, but perhaps this was the right time to think about selling the company and doing something else. Like sailing the Atlantic in my yacht perhaps and other long held ambitions for which I had never had the time or money. The company was doing well, it was well known and it seemed the right time, if there is ever a right time to give up a lifetimes work.

I let my feelings be known and they came to the attention of someone who I knew, an ex-oil company executive who had given me much support in the past and who knew the business, seemed ideal and the deal was done. Part of the deal was that I should stay on as a consultant for a year or two. This seemed a good idea, to retire gradually and I accepted. With hindsight, I don't think it was a mistake to stay on, but I did not realise how difficult it would be for me to work for someone else in what had been my company.

It was during that time that I experienced the life threatening ordeal in Sri Lanka.

There was still business to be done in Sri Lanka and I was asked to go back there and pursue enquiries. This I did and stayed in a very pleasant hotel outside of Colombo. My wife was able to come with me and all seemed serene. One evening we had a couple of drinks on the terrace before retiring and all was well. And then I developed the most violent stomach upset. Everything came up (or down, as the case may be), totally exhausted from both ends.

The hotel doctor was called, but was not very helpful. Eventually I became virtually unconscious and an ambulance was called. Thankfully I was insured and I was taken to hospital and given a private room with an attendant who slept by my bed all night. The slightest movement and he was there. As I got better he helped me to shower in the morning. I don't remember much else, but it was a near thing. My agent was convinced that I had been poisoned by the Tamils, because of my work with the Air Force, but it was difficult to see how that could have been done in the hotel.

It is important, however, in spite of all the problems, to emphasise that Sri Lanka is a wonderful country with delightful people. We were fortunate enough to see some of the country and to visit the wild game park, a lifetime experience in itself that makes everything else worthwhile.

Finally, the time came to retire completely from the business. A very sad time in many ways. A life time spent in and around aircraft and now it was to end. But not quite. My seventieth birthday was coming up and there was something cooking. My children said they were joining together and there would be a secret surprise for my birthday. No clue, except just be ready for a day out. A slight clue, not understood at the time. My second daughter's birthday card mentioned this surprise day and said, 'You will be highly delighted.' I should have realised, but I didn't. The great day arrived and the surprise was revealed. They had booked me a flying lesson at a flying school at Southampton airport. Unbelievable. A lifetime's ambition was to come true. We all trooped down to the airport well before the appointed time. I was able to pay to upgrade the trainer aircraft to a four seat version so that my wife could come with me. That left one spare seat, so I offered it to any one of my children that would like to come with me. 'No, thanks, Dad. We'll watch from here.'

So off we went. The pilot took off and climbed to cruising altitude and then handed over the controls to me, 'You have control.'

'I have control,' was the approved answer. But did I? It seemed to be going well. The pilot said I could more or less go where I liked, but obviously he was keeping a careful watch. Having worked in and around aircraft and controls, especially in those early days at Gloster Aircraft Co. I knew a little about controls and flying and was able to fly over our house on Hayling Island and my wife was busy taking photographs. I then flew over to the Isle of Wight and thoroughly enjoyed the whole experience. It was time to return. The hour's lesson was nearly up. I flew the aircraft back to Southampton, round the outer marker beacon and prepared for finals, handing over control to the instructor. And then the surprise, 'You seem to know what you're doing,' he said, 'you land it.' So I did. I lined up with the runway and carefully brought the aircraft down. The instructor was obviously keeping a close watch and he looked after the engine throttle, making sure that I was approaching at the correct speed and doing nothing silly. But I did land the aircraft myself. We made a good landing and I taxied back to the dispersal area. My wife said the only time she worried during the whole flight was the landing!

But that was it. The culmination of all my dreams. My business, built up over the years with many ups and downs had gone. I had flown and landed an aircraft. I could retire in peace. But it was not to be. I quickly became deeply involved in other projects, other ambitions. Many adventures sailing my boat across the channel, the attempted, but failed Atlantic crossing and so on. But that's another story

Index

CHAPTER